Mel Bay's

COUNTRY LEAD GUITAR

by Larry McCabe

Acknowledgements

To Liz

Thanks to the following participants:

Mike Brown—Recording
Bob Clear—Notation
Buster Wilson—Bass
Junior Barlow—Drums

Table Of Contents

Preface

Few styles of music have enjoyed the widespread and enduring popularity of the many forms of American country music. With the advent of the phonograph, country music was suddenly available to a broad audience. Through the years it has developed from the rural string bands to the raw honky-tonk of the post-war period to the slick "Nashville" sound of today.

The wonderfully infectious lure of the "pure" post-war country sounds remains with us today through the artistry of performers like George Jones, Merle Haggard, Ricky Skaggs, Loretta Lynn, Moe Bandy, George Strait and others. Essential to the style is the sideman who can deliver just the right solo - be it flashy, subdued, bluesy, twangy or jazzy - to parallel the singer's message of the joys and despairs of life.

Several hundred popular country recordings were researched to come up with the twenty-five chord progressions used in this book. Each of the progressions was found to be common to several popular songs. A solo incorporating various concepts and techniques has been written to each progression. The result is an authentic-sounding collection of country guitar solos through which various ideas may be analyzed.

The solos in this collection are intended for the guitarist who has graduated from the elementary stages of playing the instrument. For the sake of convenience, the solos are grouped by keys but need not be approached in their strict order of presentation. Have fun with them.

Main Features Of This Book

The Tape

The stereo tape available for this book allows the student to hear each solo note-for-note. The listener will hear the rhythm section play one chord progression for any given tune twice-with the lead guitar joining in the second time. The rhythm and lead parts are split in stereo for the sake of clarity.

It has been shown that both correct interpretation and rapid progress are enhanced by listening (e.g. Suzuki violin students). The author urges that the tape be used with the written materials. The student who hears the phrasing of each solo is aided in terms of rhythmic sensitivity and overall comprehension. Please use the tape, it brings the music to life.

To make the best use of the book and tape together, listen to each solo very carefully before attempting to play it. It may be helpful to pick out phrases of notes on the tape, find them in the book, then play through each phrase very carefully until the solo is memorized. Constant attention should be given to accuracy of noting and timing.

Tablature

Tablature is a system of numbers which helps the nonreader locate notes. It also helps the reader to pinpoint specific note location. An explanation of tablature may be found in the symbols section of this book.

Performance Notes

The performance notes which accompany solos provide insight as to the "why" and "how" of each solo. These comments are designed to benefit the student who desires a practical understanding of various theoretical principles.

Variations

Each solo is supplemented with a one or two measure variation which may be applied in a designated spot in the progression. The variations give the student insight as to the depth of freedom the experienced guitarist enjoys when playing in this style.

IMPORTANT! When the performance notes refer to a specific measure, the pickup measure (if there is one) is not considered to be the "first measure." "Measure one" refers to the first full measure of the progression, with the following measures numbered accordingly.

Theory and Basic Concepts in Soloing

The appendix in this book contains a brief explanation of theory as it relates to soloing. The student is urged to study this section as the principles outlined here are constantly reinforced and expanded upon in the performance notes.

Hand Charts and Melodic Exercises

The appendix contains a wealth of hand charts and melodic exercises in the following scales:

MAJOR: C, G, D, A, E
BLUES: C, G, D, A, E
PENTATONIC: A, B, C, D, E, F, G

Each chart details several common fingering positions for a given scale. Also, a melodic exercise accompanies each position scale, bringing it to life. The student who makes use of the charts will gain much insight into the fingerings and sounds of the various scales. Playing the scales and melodic exercises up and down the guitar neck is excellent for technique development.

Instant Application

The progressions in this book can be heard on many standard country recordings. A quality teacher who does a little research should be able to help the student find a great number of popular tunes which the solos may be applied to.

Additional Uses of Book

In addition to teaching lead solos, this book and tape could also be used to suit the following purposes:

OBJECTIVE	PROCEDURE
. Ear Training	. Student identifies chord progressions by ear.
. Basic chord studies	. Student strums along.
. Bass playing	. Beginning bassist writes parts to progressions.
. Improvisation	. Student writes melody parts to progressions.
. Research	. Student researches albums to match popular tunes to progressions in book.

How To Read Tablature

Tablature is a system designed to pinpoint the location of notes on the fingerboard. The tablature in this book appears directly underneath the music staff. Tablature consists of six lines, with the space above each line used in reference to a specific string.

If we wish to show the exact location of a note, we simply write the number of the fret it is found on in the appropriate (string) space. The open third string (G) is shown in the example at the left. Open strings are identified by the number "O."

When notes are "stacked" on top of one another like in the example at the left, play them all at once as you would a chord.

Fingerings

For your convenience, small numbers attached to notes in the standard notation indicate proper fretting-hand fingering.

The fretting-hand fingers are numbered as follows:

1=Index Finger 2=Middle Finger 3=Ring Finger 4=Little Finger

0=Open String.

Basic Picking Technique
Symbols: ⊓ Down-Pick ⋁ Up-Pick

Though no rules concerning picking technique are all-inclusive, the following information will help serve as a general guideline.

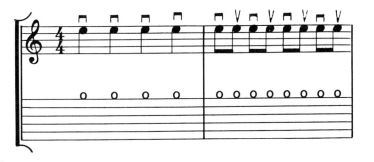

#1. Play down beats with a down-pick motion, as shown in the first measure at the left.

#2. Play up beats with an up-pick motion, as shown in the second measure at the left. Notice also that a succession of eighth notes should be played with alternate picking motions.

#3. Alternate-pick a succession of sixteenth notes, as shown in the example at the left.

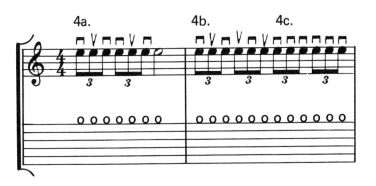

#4. Three techniques are used to pick triplets.
  #4a. Triplets may be played (⊓⋁⊓ ⊓⋁⊓) with the downpick on the first and third note of each triplet group.
  #4b. Tripltes may be alternate picked (⊓⋁⊓ ⋁⊓⋁).
  #4c. Triplets may be played with the exclusive use of the downpick (⊓⊓⊓ ⊓⊓⊓). This is especially effective for chord style rhythms which use triplets.

#5. Combining the rhythmic units. According to the above guidelines, the melodic example at the left could be picked as shown.

The importance of good pick technique

It is of vital importance that the student understands and can execute basic picking motions before attempting the solos in this book. If alternate picking is new to you and you are still playing every note with a downpick motion, you may not be adequately prepared for this book. If this is the case, it would be to your definite advantage to work through relevant subject matter to acquire the skills necessary to benefit from this book.

I suggest as excellent preparatory material any of the following:

1. Mel Bay's Modern Guitar Course, books one and two.
2. Building Right Hand Technique by Bill Bay. (Both books published by Mel Bay).
3. Learn a number of flatpick-style guitar solos.

[Mel Bay's Solo Folio # 1&2, Mel Bay's Mill's Favorite Guitar Solos]
A good teacher will help you with any of these approaches.

Symbols

Slide-up. Symbol ╱

"Sliding-up" is accomplished by the following:

1. Pick a fretted note . . . then,
2. "Slide" or move the fretting finger up the neck (without releasing finger pressure) to the next note.

The example at the left shows us to fret the D note on the second string, pick the string, then slide the first finger up from the third fret to the E note on the fifth fret.

Sliding-up without a specific "point of departure." Symbol ╱

This particular designation of a slide indicates that there is no specific "point of departure"-only a "destination." The example at the left shows us to start the slide "somewhere" on the second string (at a lower pitch on the neck than the eighth fret), stopping when the third finger reaches the eighth fret.

Slide-down. Symbol ╲

Sliding-down is the reverse of sliding-up. The example to the left shows us to pick the second string at the third fret (while fretting with the first finger) and then slide the first finger <u>back</u> to the first fret while keeping pressure on the string.

Sliding-down without a specific destination. Symbol ╲

Here, we have a specific "point of departure" but have no specific "destination." The example at left shows us to slide the G note (third beat) "down" the neck (towards the machine heads) but does not tell us "exactly" where to stop sliding.

Double-slide. Symbol ╱╲ or ╲╱

To execute a double-slide:

1. Pick a fretted note . . . , then
2. Slide the finger playing that note to another note . . . , then
3. Without picking again, slide back to the original note.
   Sometimes double-stops (notes on two strings played simultaneously) are used in double-slides.

The hammer. Symbol $\overset{H}{\frown}$ or $\underset{H}{\smile}$

To execute a hammer follow this procedure:

1. Play one note with the pick . . . then,
2. "Slam" (hammer) the indicated fretting-hand finger down on the second note (to make it sound without being picked).

In the example at left the third string is played open, then the second finger of the fretting hand strikes (hammers) at the second fret to sound the A note.

Result: one pick motion, two separate notes.

IMPORTANT: Despite this example, the hammer does not always "originate" from an open string.

Double-hammer. Symbol $\overset{H}{\frown}\ \overset{H}{\frown}$ or $\underset{H}{\smile}\ \underset{H}{\smile}$

This technique allows three separate notes to be sounded with one pick motion. Execute as follows:

1. The first note is sounded with the pick . . .
2. The second note is sounded by hammering from the first note . . .
3. Without picking again, the third note is sounded by hammering from the second note.

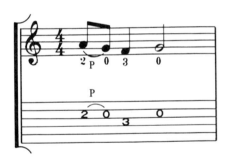

The pull-off. Symbol $\overset{P}{\frown}$ or $\underset{P}{\smile}$

The pull-off is the opposite of the hammer. The example at the left shows us to:

1. Pick the second fret of the third string . . . then,
2. "Pull" the fretting finger from the second fret in such a manner to cause the second note (here, open G) to sound. Result: one pick motion, two separate notes.

The combination hammer/pull. Symbol $\overset{H}{\frown}\ \overset{P}{\frown}$

This technique allows three separate notes to be sounded with one pick-motion. Execute as follows:

1. The first note is sounded with the pick.
2. The second note is sounded by hammering from the first note.
3. Without picking again, the third note is sounded by pulling off from the hammered note.

The double-pull Symbol

This technique allows three separate notes to be sounded with one pick-motion. Execute as follows:

1. The first note is sounded with the pick.
2. The second note is sounded by pulling from the first note.
3. Without picking again, the third note is sounded by pulling from the second note.

Repeat the two previous measures. Symbol %. Soundwise, examples #1 and #2 below are the same.

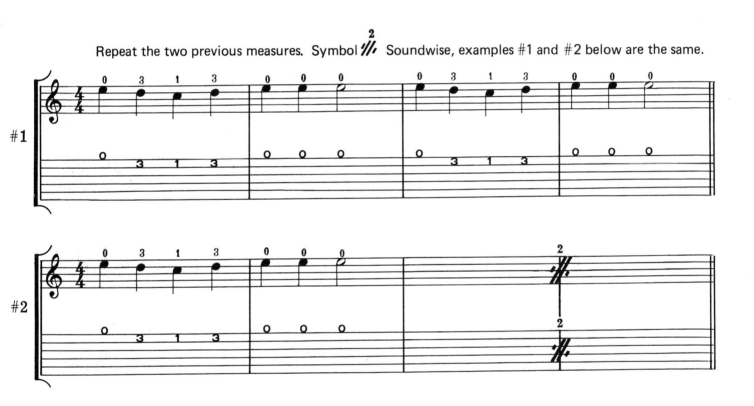

The Ottava. Symbol 8va - - - - ˥

The ottava is a symbol which helps relieve excessive use of ledger lines. When written <u>above</u> a group of notes (like in the example at the left), this sign indicates that the notes should be played an octave <u>above</u> the written pitch. Tablature is not affected by this symbol.

The Ottava. Symbol 8va_ _ _ _ _ _ _ _ _ ⌐

When written <u>beneath</u> a group of notes (like in the example at the left), this sign indicates that the notes should be played an octave <u>below</u> the written pitch. Tablature is not affected by this symbol.

String-bending
String-bending is a type of slurring technique also known as "choking", "pushing", "stretching" and "pulling." Several variants of string-bending are used in this book, each of which is detailed here.

Bend up a whole-step. Symbol ⌒
Execute a whole-step bend as follows:
1. Play the designated note in stationary position . . . then,
2. Rapidly bend (push) the string so that its pitch is raised by a whole-step (two frets).
In the example at the left, the F note is played in stationary position, then is rapidly "pushed" (toward the bass strings) with the little finger far enough to raise the pitch by a whole-step. In this example, all of this happens within the time space of half a beat. The G note in the example is then played (separately) in ordinary position on the 1 <u>and</u> beat.

Bend up a half-step. Symbol ½⌒

Follow the same procedure as for the whole-step bend up, but bend the string only far enough to raise its pitch by half a step (one fret).

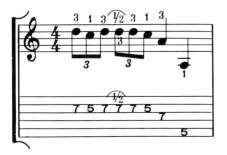

Bend down a whole-step. Symbol ⌣

The examples in the "benddown" category could also be described as "bend string, pick, and rapidly release the bend as the note is picked."
The example at the left shows us to do the following:
1. Bend the seventh fret of the third string up a whole step (pitchwise to E) . . . then,
2. Pick the note . . . then,
3. Release the bend simultaneously with the pick motion (but keep the note "alive") and restore the string to its ordinary position. This example would require a very rapid "bend down" since the affected note occupies the time space of only one-third of a beat.

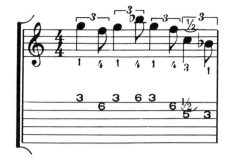

Bend down a half-step. Symbol ½

Follow the same procedure as for the whole-step bend down, but bend the string only far enough to raise its pitch by half a step (one fret) before bending down.

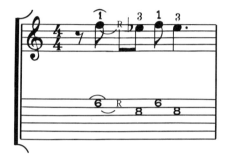

Prebend and release. Symbol ⌣ R

This bend is similar to the "bend down" except that it is not released simultaneously while picking the note. Instead, the bend is "released" over the time space of half a beat or longer.

1. "Prebend" the string the distance indicated by the symbol

2. Pick the string.
3. Release the bend (without picking again) as indicated in the notation.

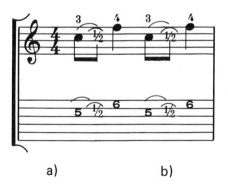

a)   b)

Notation of   Actual pitch of
whole-step   bend at its high-
bend   est point

Delayed bend up. (see example for symbol)

This bend is executed like the bend-up on page 12 but is slightly more prolonged time-wise. Illustrated, it will occupy two places (stems) in the music notation.

1. Pick the note in stationary position.
2. Without picking again, bend the note up the distance indicated by the bend symbol (⌢). Pay special attention to the notation for the proper timing of the bend.

The example at the left shows a C note being bended up to C♯.

Regarding the pitch-notation of bends.

The notation in this book shows each note according to its "fret" location on the guitar. If a note is bent, however, the actual pitch of the note will of course be higher than the pitch of the same note played in stationary position. Please look over the diagram to the left for an illustration of this point.

-Listening closely to the tape will allow you to hear the bends and will help train your ear to recognize bends from other recorded sources.

-To bend the (treble) E, B, G, and D strings, "push" them toward the bass strings.

-To bend the A and E (bass) strings, "pull" them towards the treble strings.

-It is important that you analyze the bend symbols closely and not confuse them with ties, hammers, or pulls.

Repeat an entire measure. Symbol ⅟.

This sign tells you to repeat the entire previous measure. It is used in both the notation and tablature.

Special Note Values

Grace notes. Symbol ♪

The grace note is played so rapidly that it takes up no time (theoretically) in the music. Listening closely to the tape will help you to hear the grace notes.

Stacatto notes. Symbol ♩

A <u>stacatto</u> note is sustained <u>less</u> than its written time value. Stacatto notes are often played in a rapid, sharply punctuated manner. To play a note stacatto on the guitar, release finger pressure before the note is carried through its written time value. Use your judgement and intuition concerning rapidity of release as some stacatto notes are held longer than others. <u>Stacatto</u> is a greatly popular technique among country "chicken-pickers." Stacatto markings are not written into the tablature in this book.

14

Basic Chords And Accompaniment

The forms shown here represent the basic positions of chords used in this book:

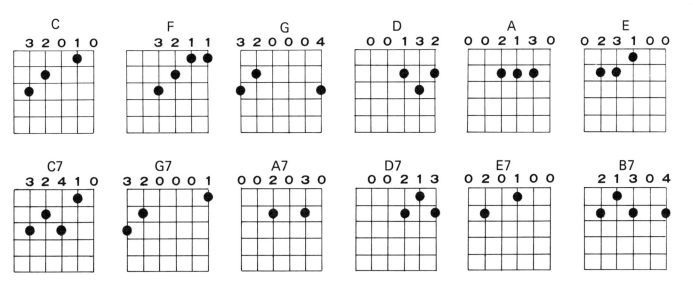

The following measures individually represent basic two-beat accompaniment for each of the above chords. Each accompaniment may be played with a pick or with the fingers. In $\frac{2}{4}$ time, the picking can be ⊓ ⊓ ⊓ ⊓ for this type of accompaniment.

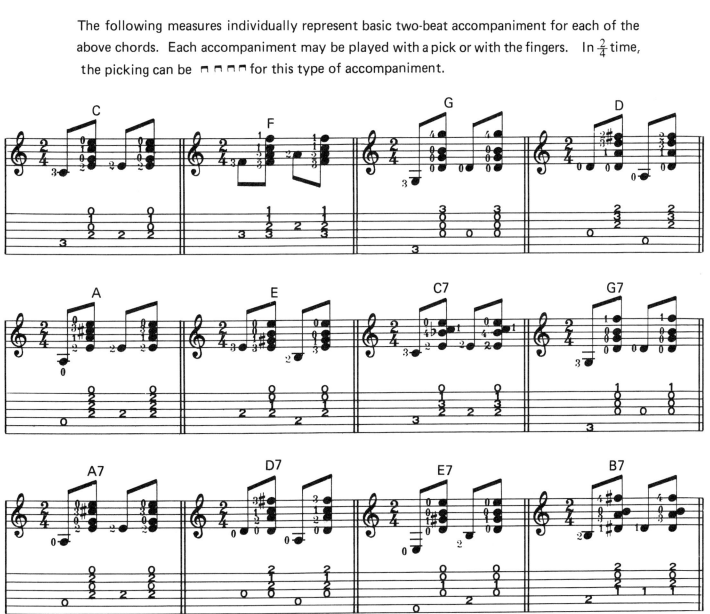

Listening Sources

Listening to as many as possible of the performers listed here is highly recommended. This will help the student hear many country sounds and fully appreciate the practical application possibilities of material in this book. Many recordings from the period of 1945-1965 are of particular relevance.

Roy Acuff - Lynn Anderson - Moe Bandy - Johnny Cash - Patsy Cline - Tommy Collins - Commander Cody - Jimmy Dickens - Lefty Frizzell - Merle Haggard and The Strangers - Emmylou Harris - Waylon Jennings - George Jones - Loretta Lynn - Rose Maddox - Willie Nelson - Buck Owens and The Buckaroos - Dolly Parton - Ray Price - Jim Reeves - Ricky Skaggs - Carl Smith - Hank Snow - Red Steagall - Wynn Stewart - George Strait - Hank Thompson - Ernest Tubb - Conway Twitty - Porter Wagoner - Gene Watson - Kitty Wells - Don Williams - Hank Williams - Tammy Wynette - Faron Young —And many others

* Much of this solo is based on the pentatonic scale. See appendix for analysis of this scale.

* The notes in measures 1-2, 7-9, 13, and 15-16 are all taken from the C pentatonic scale (c-d-e-g-a) and are played over the accompanying chord C.

* The notes in measure ten are from the C pentatonic scale except for the B$\flat$ note which belongs to the accompanying chord C7 (c-e-g-b$\flat$).

* Measures eight and fourteen are rhythmically phrased in a manner which gives us a break from the lengthy "barrage" of sixteenth notes which preceded them.

* The notes in measures 11-12 are all taken from the F pentatonic scale (f-g-a-c-d) and are played over the accompanying chord F.

Melodic Variation

This variation belongs in measure twelve and is based on the F pentatonic scale.

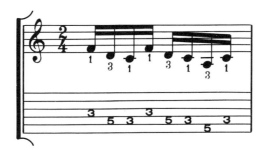

675-9913

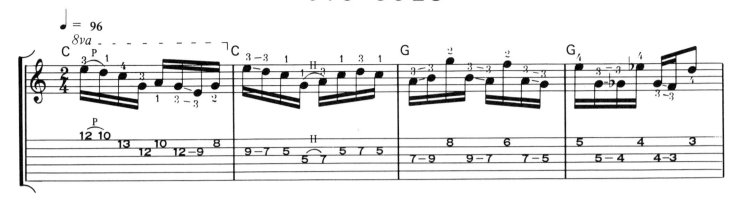

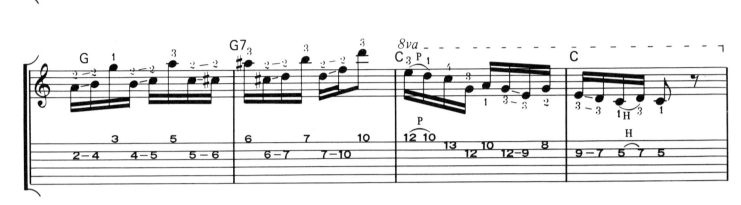

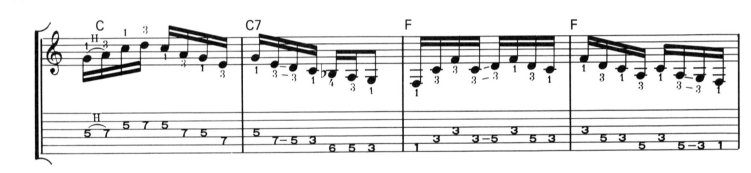

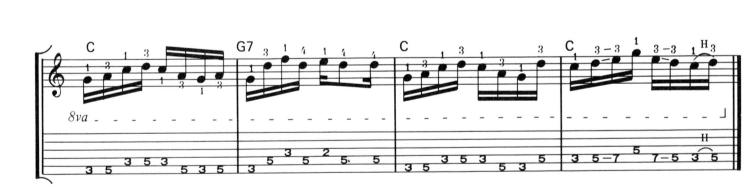

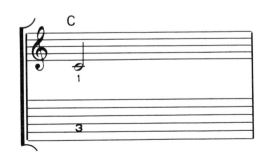

Pink Tiger

* This solo uses "pattern" fingerings in which short melodic phrases are repeated in correspondence to the accompanying chord.

* The flatted seventh note of the C scale (B♭) is used in measure two as an element of its accompanying C7 chord (c - e - g - b♭).

* The flatted seventh note of the F scale (E♭) is "forced" against the F major chord (f - a - c) in measure four and creates a straining, discordant "bluesy" sound. This concept is used quite regularly by country guitarists.

* The idea in measure eight is much the same as the idea used in measure fifteen of "Coastin." In each case, the idea is used over the V7 chord (G7) just before switching to the I chord (C).

* Be sure to use the middle finger of the picking hand where indicated by the symbol _m_ .

Melodic Variation

Use this idea in the second measure. A rapid shift of the fretting hand is required to get to the last note.

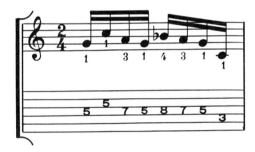

Pink Tiger

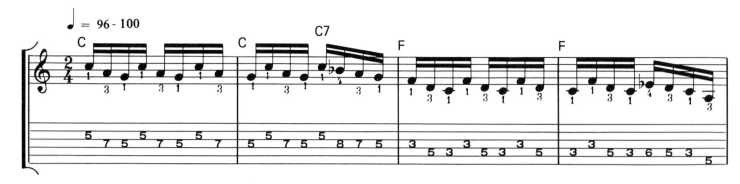

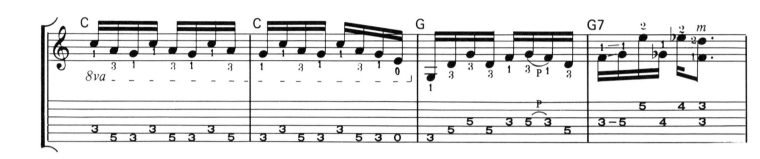

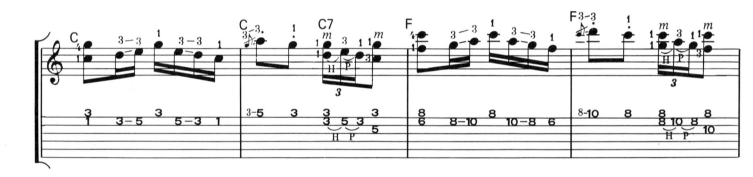

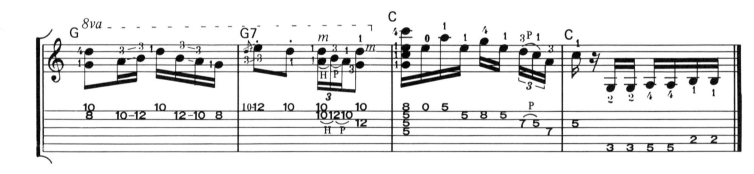

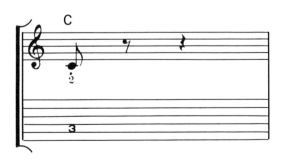

Fire In My Heart

* The pickup notes should be played stacatto (cut short) using downpicking.

* Many bends and slides are used in this solo, giving it a steel guitar-like characteristic. Each slurring technique is described in the symbols section of this book.

* The final note in measure four (b) "anticipates" the G chord (g - b - d) in measure five. Melodically, this concept can be applied to many circumstances by simply playing a note belonging to the chord which comes next immediately before the chord change is made. (Another way to use anticipation is to play the chord itself momentarily before it is "supposed" to be played, but that is another subject.)

* Notice the phrasing (following the anticipation) in measures 5-6.

* The melodic phrase in measures 9-10 is the same one that was used in measures 7-8. This is often called "repetition of a motive." Note that the same idea is repeated in measures 11-12 but is adjusted to correspond to the F chord.

* Measure thirteen begins with the same idea used in measure one.

Melodic Variation

Use this variation in measures 9-10. Notice that the B♭ note fits right in with the C7 chord (c - e - g - b♭) in measure ten.

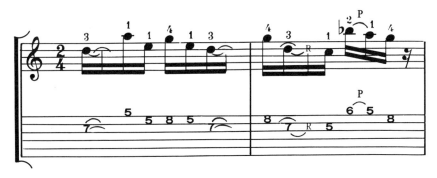

Fire In My Heart

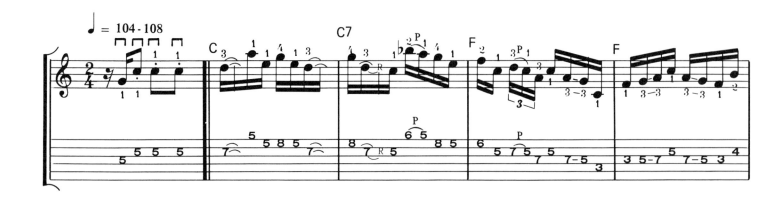

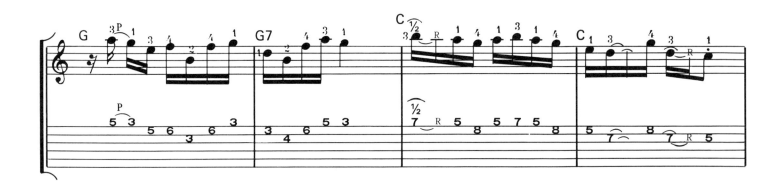

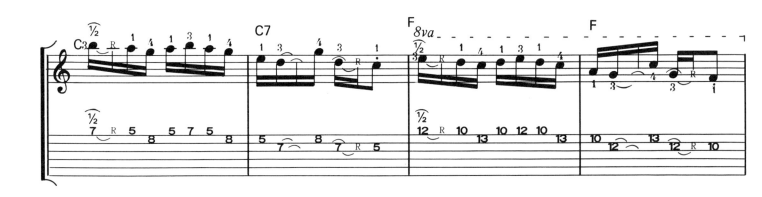

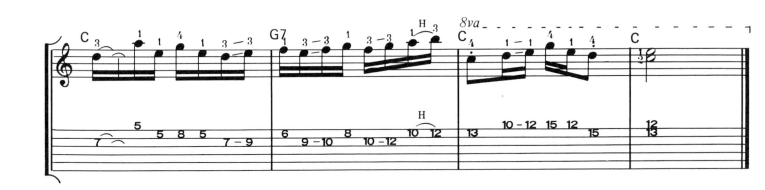

Coastin'

* Note that the pickup notes are also used to end the solo.

* Note that the non-diatonic note B♭ in measure two corresponds to the accompanying chord C7 (c-e-g-b♭).

* Note the use of the open-string chord tone E in measure two.

* With the exception of the double-stops in measures five and sixteen, the middle finger should be used (with an upward motion of the fingernail) to pick the higher voice of all double-stops in this solo. It should also be used to pick the individual notes labeled with a small _m_ .

* "Rake" the pick rapidly downward across the first three strings to play the double-stops beginning measures five and sixteen. In each instance, mute the second string by leaning a finger of the fretting hand against it.

* Measures 5-7 each consist of a one-octave descending diatonic run. Each run originates from a tone of its accompanying chord G (g-b-d) or G7 (g-b-d-f).

* The run in measure seven leads us to the E note in measure eight in which the C chord (c-e-g) appears. Melodic ideas will "revolve" around or sound complimentary with the accompanying chord while "tying together" the overall chord progression.

* If desired, the first note in each of measures 5-7 may be accented. Melodic phrases are often enhanced through the appropriate use of accenting.

* The first half of this solo is based primarily on the C major scale. Of course, provision is made for the non-diatonic chord C7, and in certain instances accidentals are used elsewhere as well.

* The second half of the solo relies heavily on the C blues scale. Thus, we are theoretically permitted to "mix" various types of scales over the same chord progression. As always, the ear is the final judge regarding quality of application.

Melodic Variation

This idea may be used beginning in the seventeenth and final measure. Note that it "leads us back" into the first measure of the progression.

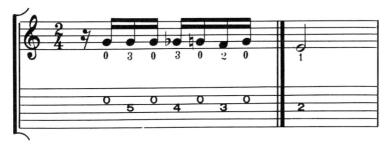

Coastin'

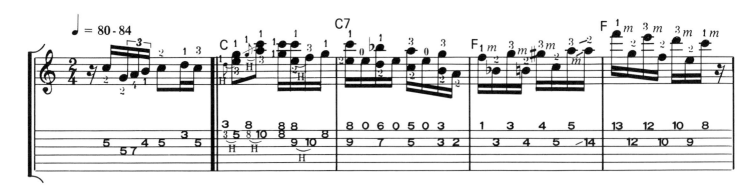

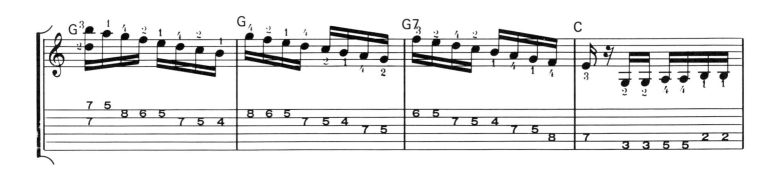

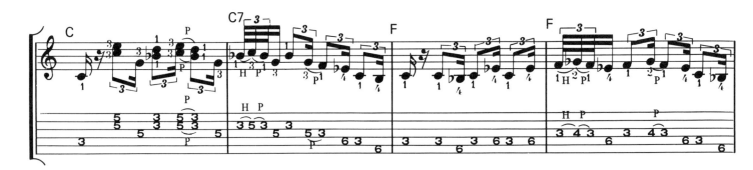

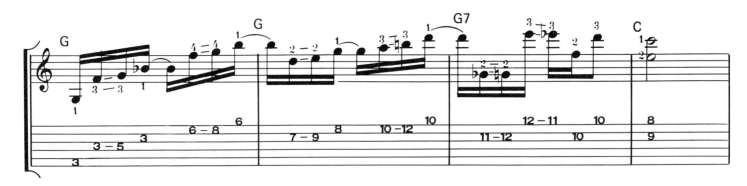

(first measure
of progression)

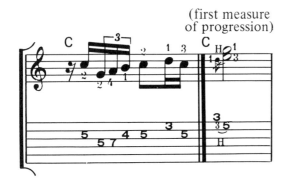

Flying While Using A Doghouse For Wings

* Note that only the I (C) and V (G or G7) chords are used in this progression. Still, there is much opportunity to create a solo, and we need not feel restricted by the small number of chords.

* The pickup idea in this solo is suitable for use in many solos, and it often works well as a solo-closing statement.

* Alternate picking is necessary throughout this solo.

* The extensive use of the fourth finger--along with the many position shifts--makes this an excellent exercise for the fretting hand.

* Many chromatic (non-diatonic) notes are used in this solo. The following examples demonstrate a few ways chromatic tones may be used:

The last note in measure two, E♭ , is a non-diatonic note. It is found "between" tones of two adjacent chords in the progression (C and G) and "links" a tone (e) of the C chord in measure two to a tone (d) of the G chord in measure three.

Often, chromatic notes function as passing tones which "connect" two tones of the accompanying chord. In measure six, the G♭ note "connects" the G note chord tone to the F note chord tone. Each chord tone is contained in the accompanying chord G7 (g-b-d-f).

When a chromatic note is used to "connect" two diatonic notes, it is not always necessary that either or both of the diatonic notes belong to the accompanying chord. In measure 14 a G♯ note is used to connect G to A, yet only the G note itself belongs to the accompanying chord, G (g-b-d). In the same measure an A♯ note is used to connect A to B, yet only the B note is in the G chord.

Sometimes a chromatic will be played a half-step above or below a chord tone, then the chord tone itself is played again. Measure one contains an example of this. The F♯ note follows the G note (belonging to the accompanying C chord c-e-g); the G note is then played again, after the F♯ . Can you locate this concept elsewhere in the solo?

* Soundwise, chromatic notes should always be used in a purposeful manner.

Melodic Variation

Use this variation in measure ten as an alternative means of using a chormatic (here, C♯) to "link" a C chord tone (c) to a G chord tone (d).

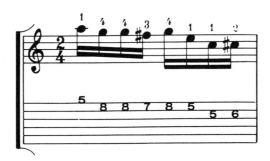

Flying While Using A Doghouse For Wings

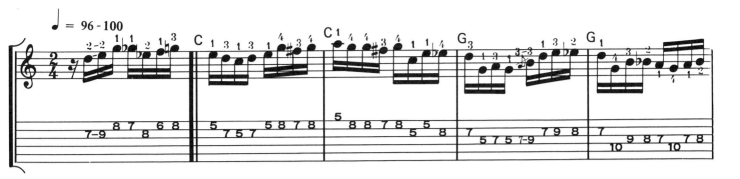

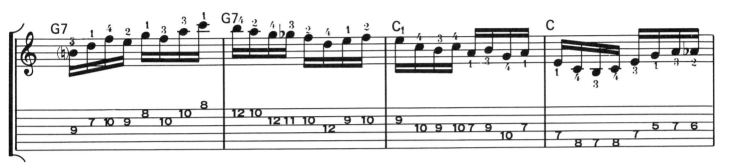

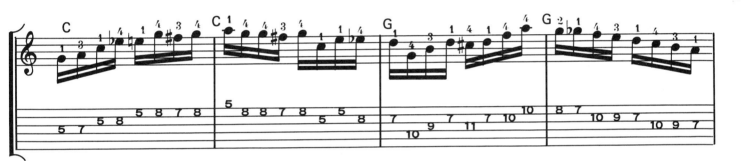

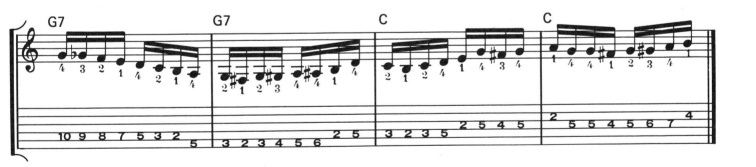

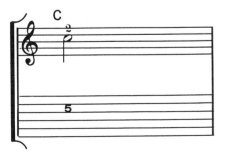

Octopus

* There are only eight measures in this progression. Only the I (G) and V7 (D7) chords are used. Many country fiddle tunes are based on a single eight-bar progression, or two sections each consisting of an eight-bar progression.

* This entire solo is played in the seventh position.

* Note that the rhythmic phrasing in bars 3-4, 5-6 and 7-8 is the same.

* Note the various usage of accidentals in this solo.

Melodic Variation

Use this "fiddle" lick in the third and/or seventh measures.

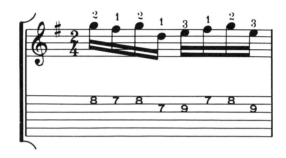

Navy Blues

* Note the use of the twelve-bar progression here. Many "country blues" musicians such as the late Moon Mullican used this type of progression often.

* The G blues scale (G-B♭ -C-C♯ -D-F) is the tonal basis for this solo.

* Note that the open string tones G and D in measure two each belong to the accompanying chord G (g, b, d).

* Note the syncopated, ascending blues scale melodic idea used in measures 4-6.

* Use the fretting hand thumb to fret the bass G note in measure eleven.

* In this type of progression it is common for the I chord to be played as a I7 throughout. For example, G7 could be used in measures 1-4, 7-8, and 11-12.

For more information on 12-bar blues (and many solos),
see my book "Blues, Boogie and Rock Guitar," Mel
Bay Publications.

Melodic Variation

This variation may be used in measures 10-11.

29

Navy Blues

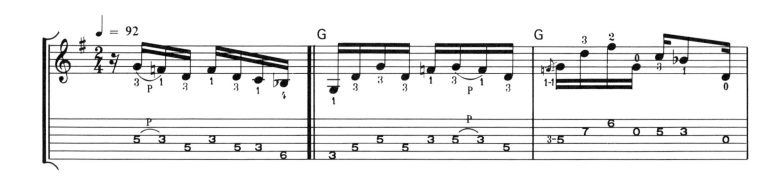

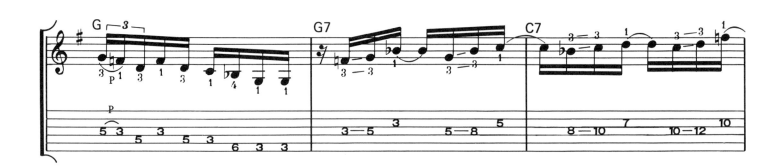

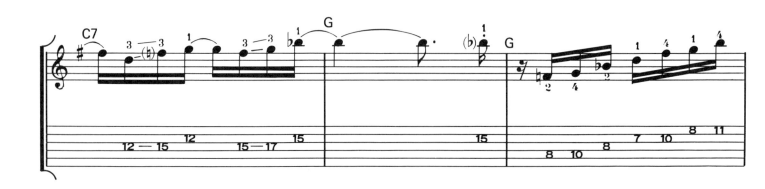

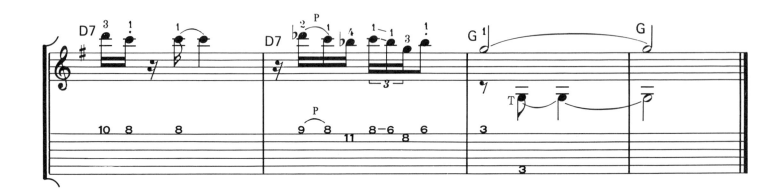

Black Wolf

* The three-note melodic concept in measures 1-2 is copied in measures 3-4 with a new set of notes to adjust to the new chord.

* The flatted seventh tone B♭ is "forced" against the C major chord (c-e-g) in measures 3-4 and 11-12 to create a "bluesy" effect.

* The four-beat "walking octave" idea in measures 7-8 originates on the root of the accompanying chord D (d-f♯-a) and proceeds upward to its destination on the F♯ note which is the third of the chord. This melodic idea can be used over and over in country lead work.

* In the sixteenth measure, the open G string acts as a root drone note to the chromatic descension which leads from the D note to the B note (reminder: the G chord is made of the notes g-b-d).

Melodic Variation

Use this G pentatonic (g-a-b-d-e) idea in measures one and two.

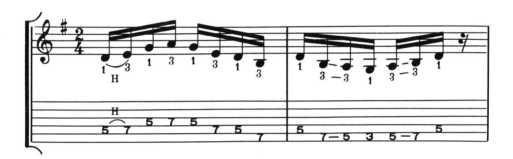

Black Wolf

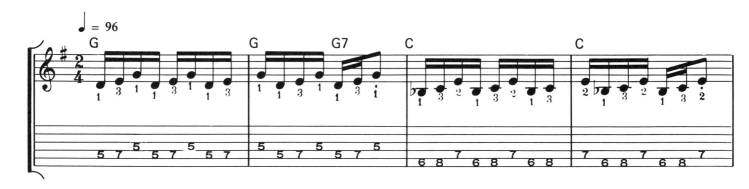

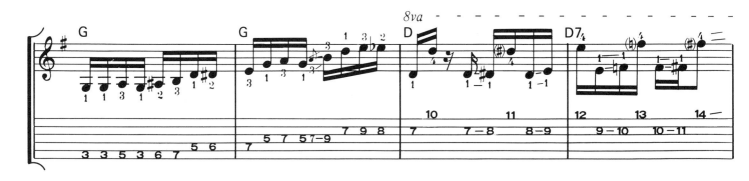

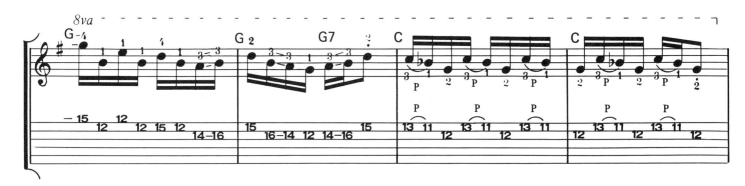

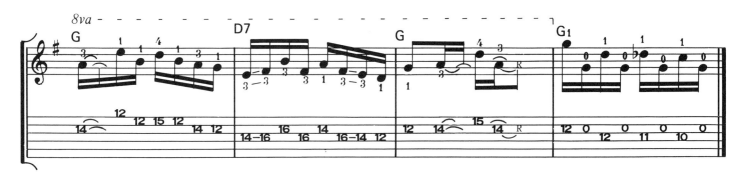

Neon Jungle

* The first six bars of the solo are based on the G pentatonic scale (g-a-b-d-e).

* The phrase in measures 7-8 is comprised of four separate "staggered" descending diatonic runs of four notes each. We say "staggered" because the entire phrase does not descend in a straight line, but is fragmented into four short "blocks" of four notes each. Beginning with the second "block" of notes, each block originates from a note one scale degree lower than the first note in the block of notes which preceded it. Please note that the phrase originates on the A note of the accompanying chord D (d-f♯-a) and leads to the D note of the G chord (g-b-d) in measure nine.

* A rapid hand shift from the fourth to the second position is required in measure eight.

* Measures 9-10 (G chord, g-b-d) and measures 11-12 (C chord, c-e-g) use the concept of "staggered" descending diatonic runs which was used in measures 7-8. Note that in all <u>three</u> instances the two-bar phrase originated from the fifth of the accompanying chord.

* Note the use of the ascending idea in measures 13-14.

Melodic Variation

Use this idea in measures 7-8. Note the use of the accidentals.

Neon Jungle

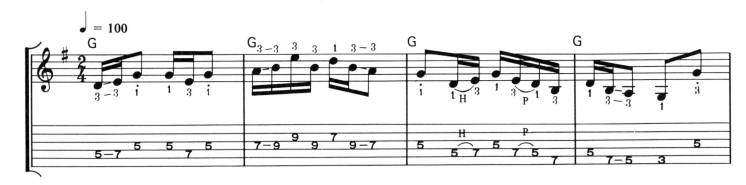

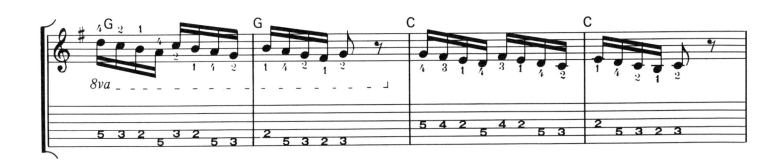

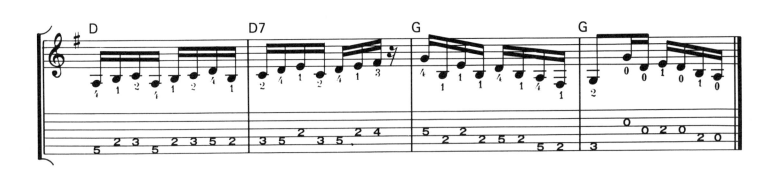

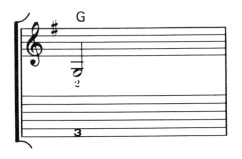

Admit Two

* This progression uses only the I (G) and V (D or D7) chords.

* The B bass note in measures 1-3 may be allowed to ring.

* The F♯ bass note in measures 4-7 may be allowed to ring.

* This solo contains the use of much <u>crosspicking.</u> In general, crosspicking refers to a method of pattern picking in which flatpick-style "rolls" are played using three adjacent strings. Often, a "fixed" fretting hand position is held on the strings to form an arpeggio made of notes belonging to the accompanying chord. Also, it is common for notes to be "added" to the arpeggio, as you will see in this solo.

* Notice the relationship, concept-wise, of measures 4-7 (D chord) to measures 1-3 (G chord). In each instance, the picking was initiated on the <u>third</u> of the accompanying chord (i.e., the B note of the G chord; the F♯ note of the D chord) and then continued downward across the next two open strings (which in each case also belonged to the accompanying chord). Each melodic idea was then completed by adding notes to the basic arpeggio position.

* The "double hammer" technique used in measure eight is described in the symbols section of this book.

* Melodically, the run in measure eight is known as the "G-run" or the "Flatt run" in reference to its frequent use in the bluegrass style of the late Lester Flatt.

* Measures 9-16 have the same chord progression as measures 1-8. The melodic ideas in each section could be considered as being alternative ways of approaching the same eight-bar progression.

* Measures 10-12 find us once again using the crosspicking technique. The open G string in measure ten gives us a banjo-like sound.

* Measure eleven requires the index finger of the fretting hand to form a "half-barre" across the seventh fret of the first three strings.

* The phrase in measures 13-15 descends in a "staggered" method (using four-note diatonic groupings) from the A note of the accompanying chord D (d-f♯-a) and leads us to the root of the G chord (g-b-d) which appears in measure 16.

* The solo-closing idea (beginning in measure sixteen) is applied elsewhere in this book. Can you find an example?

Melodic Variation
Use this variation for measure three. The open strings may be allowed to ring.

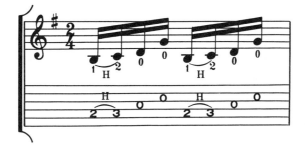

Admit Two

♩ = 100

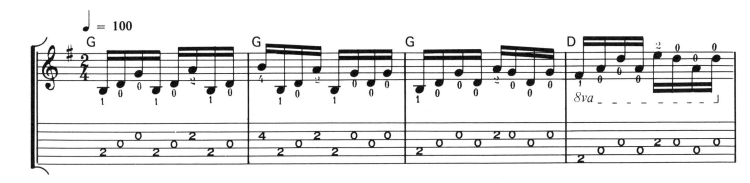

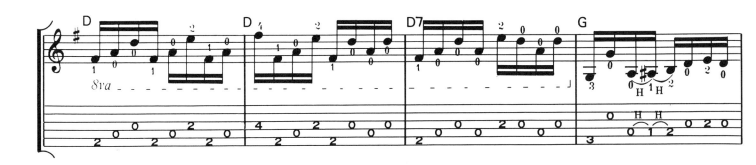

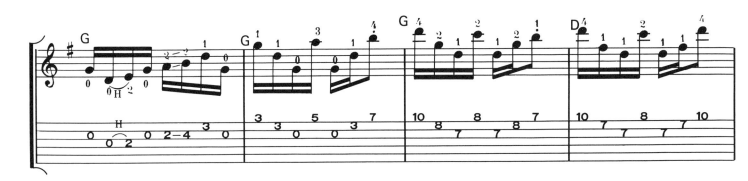

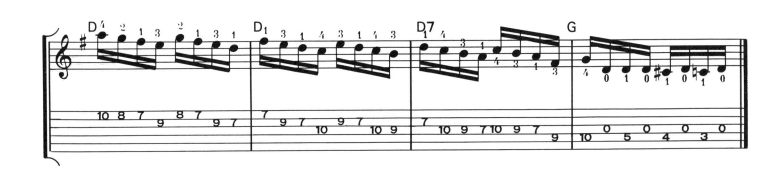

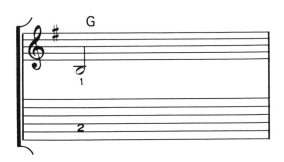

Blues For Earl Haywood

* This solo is based on the D blues scale (d, f, g, g♯, a, c) and has a sort of "rockabilly" sound.

* Note the hand shift in measure two.

* Measures 5-6 are the same as measures 1-2 in the sense that the notes are the same. Also, the accompanying chord to each set of measures is the same (D). Yet, the notes in measures 1-2 begin a phrase which is accompanied entirely by a D chord (mes. 1-4) while the notes in measures 5-6 begin a phrase which goes from a D chord to an A7 chord (mes. 5-7).

* All three slides in measure fourteen are played with the first finger.

* Note the use of the double pull-off in measure sixteen. This technique was also used in "Coastin'" in the key of C.

Melodic Variation

This idea may be used in measure eight.

Blues For Earl Haywood

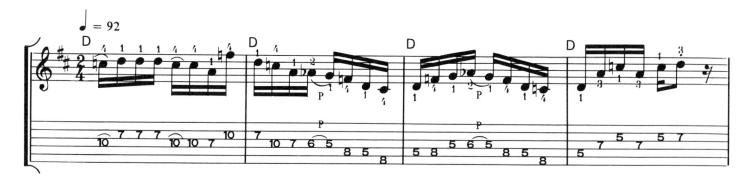

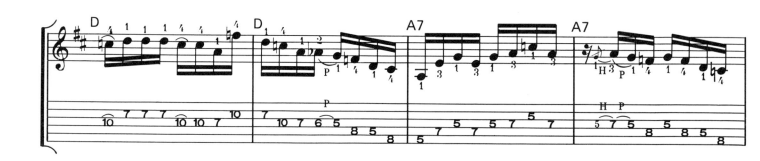

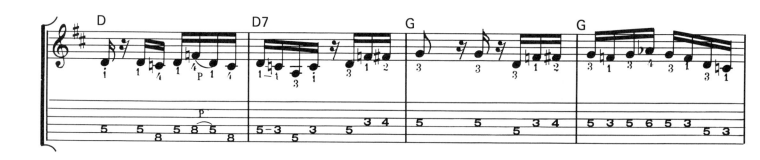

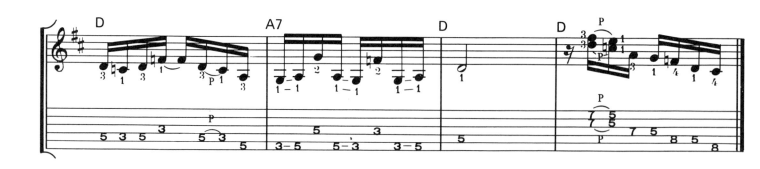

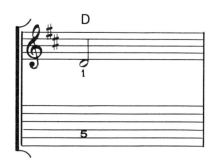

Anger Amongst The Teapots

* The entire solo should be muffled by resting the side of the picking hand on the strings near the bridge. If you wish, muting can also be accomplished by putting a snug-fitting sponge or piece of foam rubber under the strings.

* If desired, a little extra reverb may be used for this solo.

* The idea starting in the first measure originates from the C♯ tone or major seventh tone of the accompanying D chord. Up to this point, most major chord runs in this book have originated from a note in the basic triad of the accompanying chord.

* The idea used in measure eleven (and continuing to the first note in measure twelve), although played to a G chord, contains no tones from the G triad (g, b, d). The two main tones used here are the major seventh (f♯) and the major sixth (e) of the G chord. By branching out and using tones like major sixths and major sevenths to build lead ideas we open the door to greater creative potential.

Melodic Variation

Use this variation for measure fourteen.

Anger Amongst The Teapots

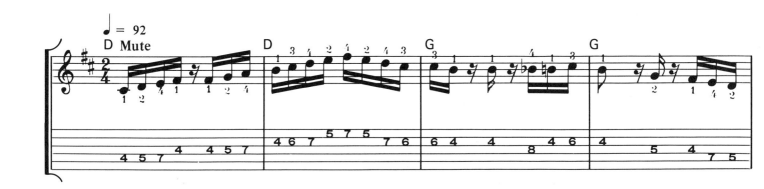

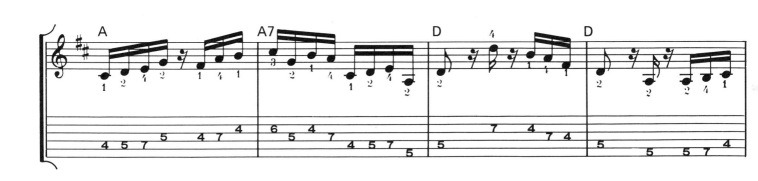

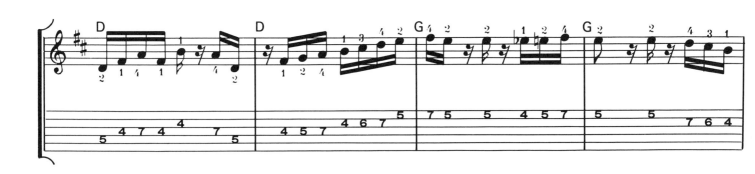

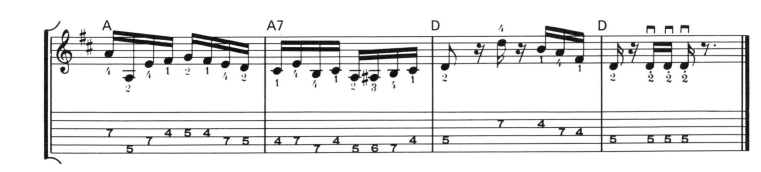

1130 Grand Avenue

* Note the lower-string use in measures 1-8.

* Measures 3-4 contain the same idea as measures 1-2 except that the idea is adjusted to "fit" the A chord (mes. 3-4).

* The lick in measures 5-6 is simply an idea using tones from the accompanying A7 chord (a, c♯, e, g).

* Note the long (5-fret) slide which connects measures ten and eleven.

* Note the use of the non-diatonic ♭7 note F as used against its accompanying chord G (g, b, d) in measures 11-12. Conceptually, the arpeggio idea used here is very similar to the idea used in measures 5-6.

* The last note in measure fourteen (E) "anticipates" the A chord (in measure fifteen) by 1/4 of a beat.

* The lick ending the solo may be found elsewhere in this book. See "Coastin'" (Key of C) and "Admit Two" (Key of G) for examples.

Melodic Variation

This idea is used in measures 5-6. Notice that this is simply a "climbing" type of arpeggio using tones from the accompanying A7 chord (a, c♯, e, g).

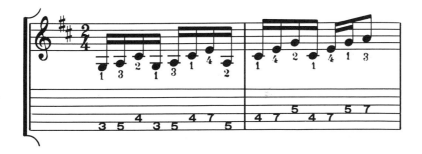

1130 Grand Avenue

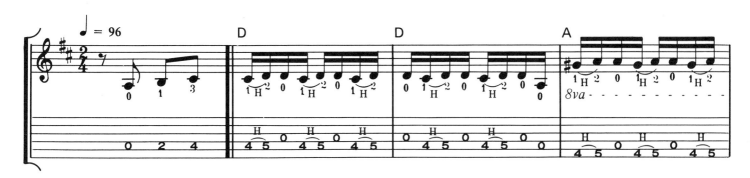

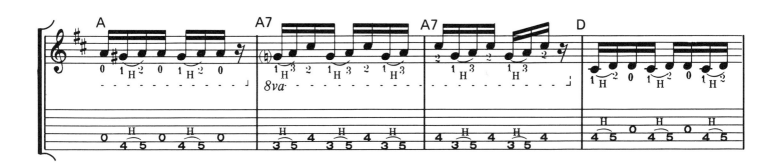

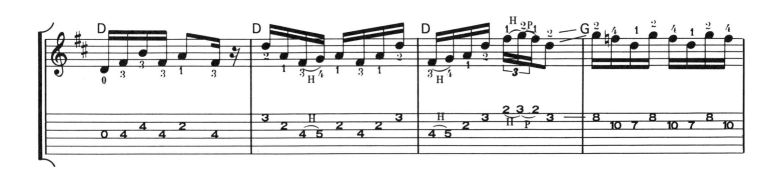

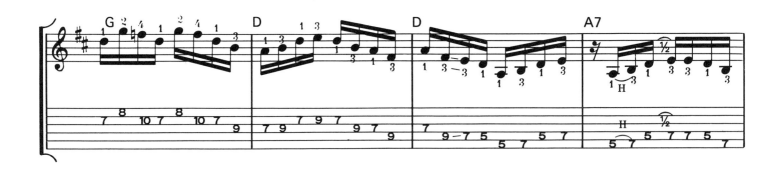

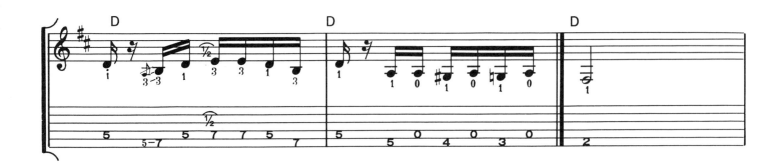

Hootowl Howls Tonight

* Each of the down-bends in measure one "originates" on a non-diatonic "blue" note. The first down-bend originates on the flatted third note (F) and the second down-bend originates on the flatted seventh note (C).

* Measure two is a repetition of measure one only is played an octave lower.

* The non-diatonic E7 chord is used in measures 3-4 and 11-12. A non-diatonic <u>chord</u> is one which contains one or more notes not in the key of the song it is being used in.

* Crosspicking (described in "Admit Two" in the key of G) is used in measures 3-6 and 11-12.

* Measures 11-12 are a repetition of measures 3-4 except that they are played an octave higher.

* The phrase in measures 13-14 originates on the root (A) of the accompanying chord, A (a, c♯, e), and descends diatonically to the F♯ note which begins measure 15. Note that the F♯ belongs to its accompanying chord D (d, f♯, a).

Melodic Variation

Use this variation in measures 9-10. The first finger should not "jump" back and forth between the A and E notes but should remain "fixed" across the fifth fret, requiring no more than a slight roll of the finger to get from one note to another.

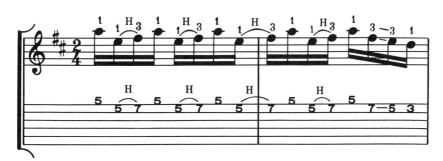

Hootowl Howls Tonight

Barbequed Polecat

* The sixteenth-note triplet in measure two contains a pull-off from the fourth finger. It may be desirable to isolate this measure in order to work this out smoothly.

* Note the lick in measure nine which originates on the b7 (g) note of its accompanying chord A7 (a, c♯ , e, g).

* Note that the rhythmic phrasing of measures 9-10 and 11-12 is the same.

* Note the "climbing" effect caused by the phrase in measures 13-14 which is based mainly on intervals of a third. Note that two position shifts are required to play this phrase.

Melodic Variation

Use this variation in measure six. Note the use of the passing tone D♯ .

Barbequed Polecat

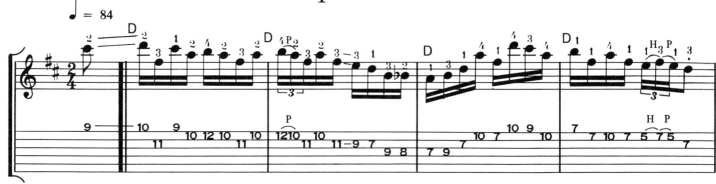

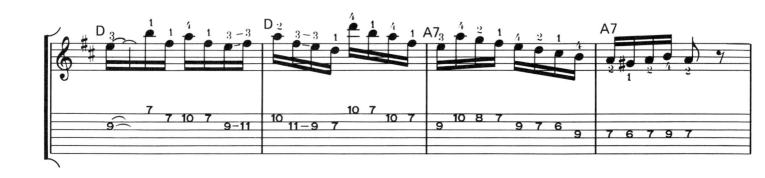

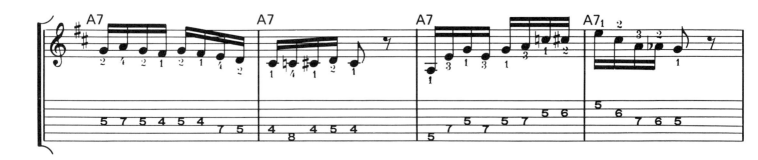

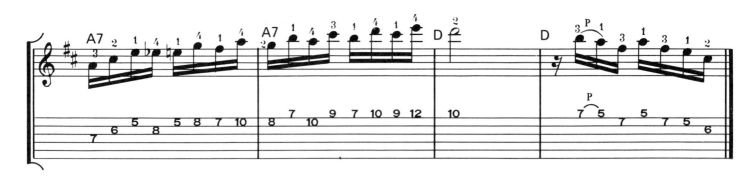

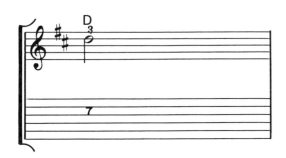

The Spacewalk

* This solo is played through an echo-delay unit.

* This solo will give you a good view of various A scale positions.

* Measure two requires the flattening out of the second finger of the fretting hand across the three consecutive notes on the 12th fret.

* Runs originating from the major sixth tone of their accompanying major chord scale are found in measures three and five.

* There are many one-octave diatonic runs based off chord tones in this solo (see measures 6, 13, 14, 15, 16). Follow the fingerings closely and be sure to analyze the theoretical implication behind each run.

Melodic Variation

Use this one-octave diatonic descending phrase in measure six.

The Spacewalk

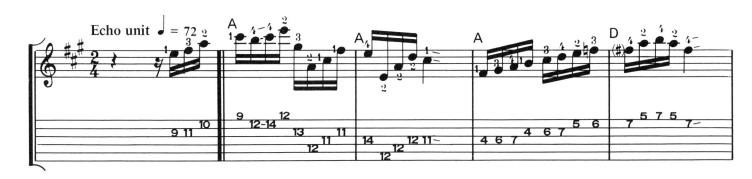

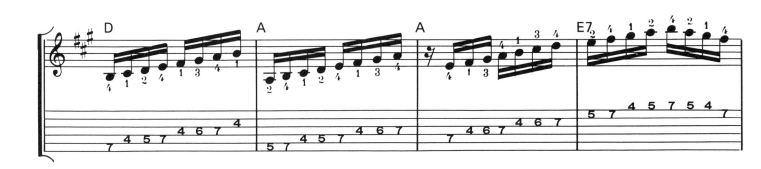

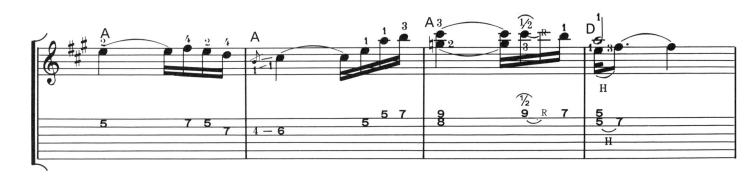

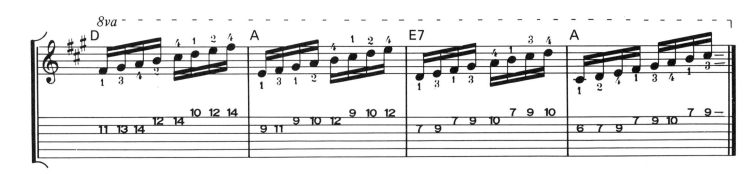

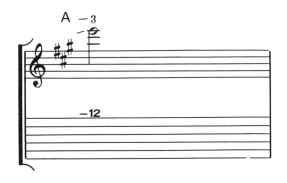

Fishin' On The Bottom

* This progression has eighteen bars. The lead work is in a sort of "truckdriving" style which makes frequent use of blue notes and bass strings.

* The lead idea in measure one (extending into measure two) may also be found in "1130 Grand Avenue" in the key of D.

* Note the use of the open-string root (A) in measures 1-2.

* The final note in measure four (B) anticipates the E chord (e, g♯, b) which appears in measure five.

* Note the use of the flatted third of the A scale (C) as applied against the E7 chord in measure seven (it is used again in measure sixteen).

Melodic Variation

Use this variation in measure four.

Fishin' On The Bottom

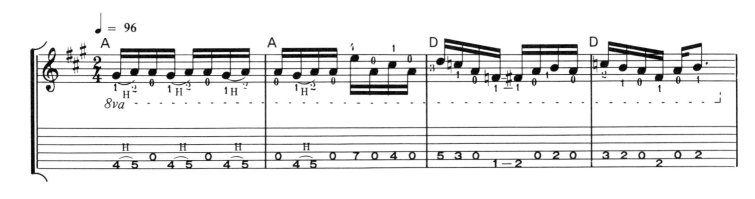

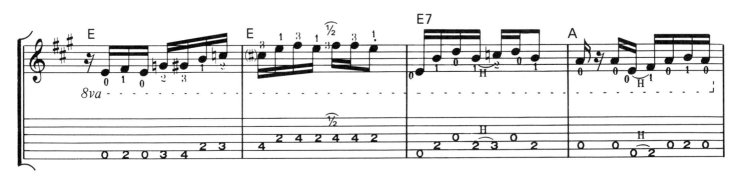

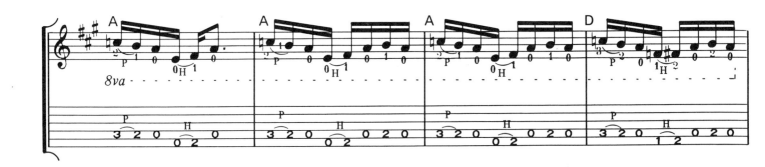

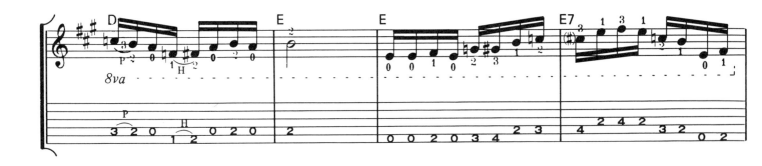

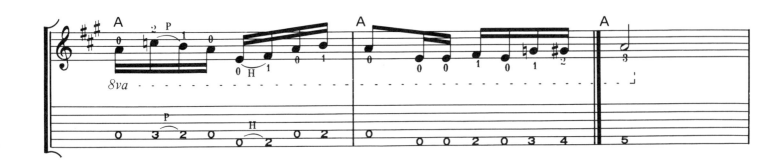

Exit 4

* The pickup idea for this solo was also used in "Flying While Using a Doghouse for Wings" in the key of C.

* Note the arpeggio idea played to the accompanying A chord (a-c♯ -e) in measures 1-2.

* The arpeggio concept is carried into measures 3-4 to the accompanying D chord (d - f♯ - a). Note, however, that the flatted seventh of the D scale (C) is "forced" against the major harmony to create a bluesy sound (the same concept is repeated in measures 11-12).

* The open E string in measures 5-6 makes it easier to play the notes stacatto than they would be if the E note was played on the second string, fifth fret.

* Follow the fingerings closely for the crosspicking E7 roll in measure seven.

* The melodic idea in measure thirteen (played over the accompanying A chord) is based on the A pentatonic scale (a, b, c♯ , e, f♯).

* The melodic idea in measure fourteen (played over the accompanying E chord) is based on the E pentatonic scale (e, f♯ , g♯ , b, c♯).

* Note that the tonic A chord changes to the IV chord, D, following the completion of the pattern. The appearance of the IV chord as used in this fashion normally represents a shift to a different section of the song (such as finishing a verse and beginning a chorus). When this happens, our melodic ideas must provide smooth transition from one section to the next by linking the chords together.

Melodic Variation

Use this variation in measures 1-2. Be sure to follow the fingerings closely.

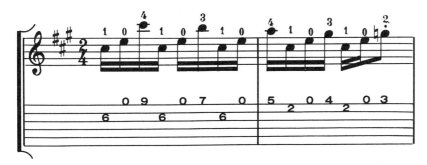

Exit Four

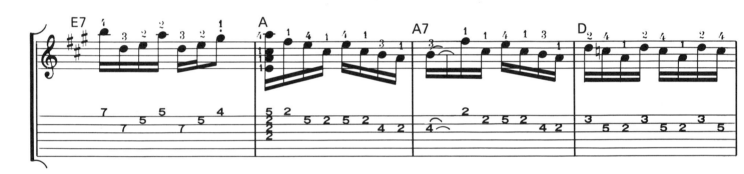

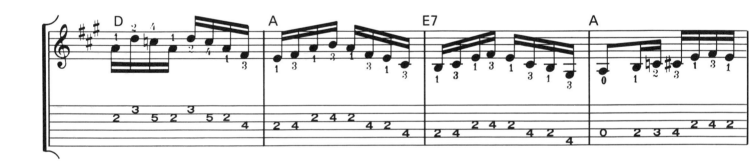

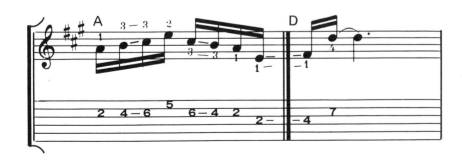

Rumble In The Chicken House

* Much of this solo is played stacatto to give a "chicken pickin" effect. Stacatto notes should be played with a heavy pick attack while releasing finger pressure (but not contact) from the fretted note immediately after picking.

* The use of the open string G note (the flatted seventh of the accompanying A chord) in measure one creates a "bluesy" sound.

* The open string D in measure three is the root of the accompanying chord. The concept of using a chord root in open-string fashion (as a sort of drone note) is also found in measures four, seven, eleven, twelve and thirteen.

* Note that the rhythm section stops for two measures beginning on the first beat of the eighth measure during the solo.

* Note the use of the blue notes C, G, and D♯ (taken from the A blues scale a, c, d, d♯ , e, g,) against the accompanying A chord in measure nine. The C note is used again against the A chord in measure sixteen.

* Note the use of the open string E which is a tone from the accompanying A chord (a, c♯ , e) in measure nine.

* Instructions for all the types of bends used in this solo may be found in the symbols section at the front of the book.

Melodic Variation

Use this variation in measure four.

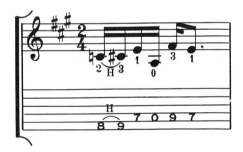

53

Rumble In The Chicken House

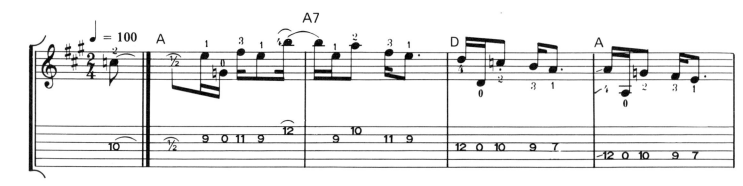

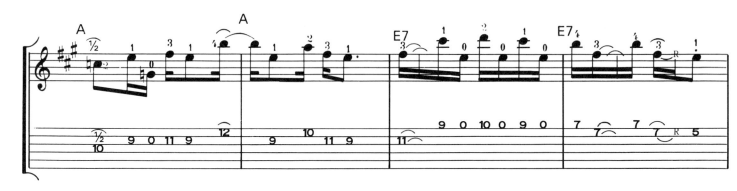

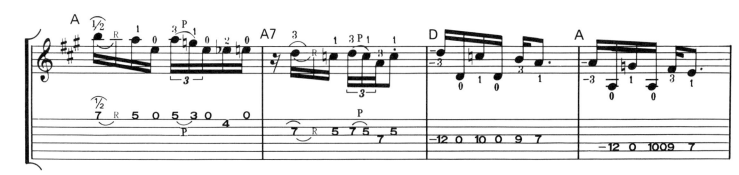

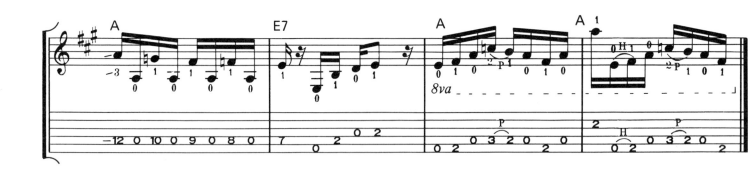

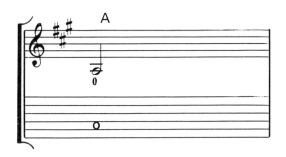

Mucho Stretcho

* An A <u>chromatic</u> scale (the chromatic scale consists of twelve successive semitones) is used in ascending fashion in measures one and two.

* A sudden hand shift in the fourth measure is used to play the last two notes in proper position and set up the slide into the fifth measure.

* Crosspicking is used in measures 5-6.

* The index finger should form a "half barre" across the fourth fret of the first three strings in measure six.

* The C note in measure eight represents the augmented fifth of the accompanying E7 chord. Augmented fifth tones are often used in melody and/or the accompanying chord itself, just before moving up a fourth chordwise (e.g., E chord to A chord).

* An unorthodox stretch is required in measure nine. The open string in the measure gives the fretting hand temporary relief.

* Note the use of the flatted seventh tone G in measure ten as it relates to its accompanying chord A7 (a, c♯ , e, g). Note also the use of the augmented fifth F note used in the same measure just before moving up a fourth chordwise from A7 to D.

* Note the strong use of the major sixth (B) and major seventh (C♯) tones as played over their accompanying D chord in measure eleven.

* The sustained tone (F♯) in measure twelve belongs to its accompanying chord D (d- f♯ -a).

* Note the way the A scale tones are utilized in a staggered, descending fashion to build the ideas making up the first three beats of measures 13-14. Note that the notes in the second half of measure fourteen then continue downward (scalewise) to link the E7 chord to the root of the A chord in measure 15.

Melodic Variation

Use this crosspicking variation for measures 5-6.

55

Mucho Stretcho

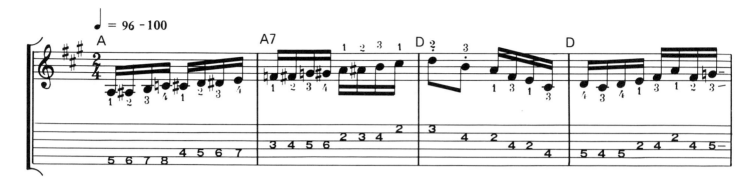

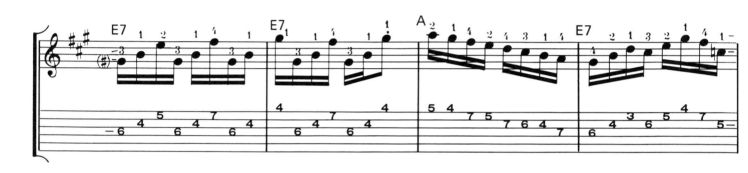

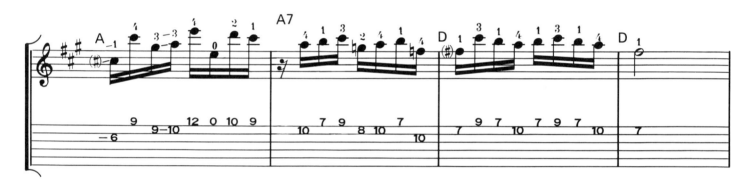

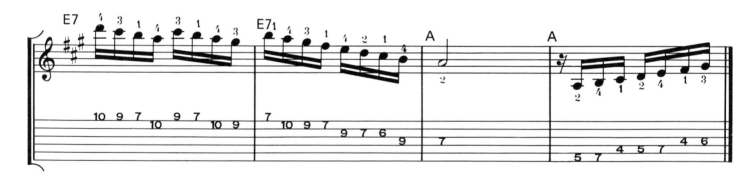

Oklahoma Stinger

* This solo demonstrates a rockabilly style of playing involving the use of double-stops.

* It is permissible to use all down-pick motions in this solo.

* The phrase from the pickup measure through measure four descends one full octave. Except for the flatted seventh D note in measures 2-3, all notes in this phrase are diatonic to the key of E. Note that the double-stops are harmonized in thirds.

* Be sure to follow fingerings and slur symbols closely.

* The idea in measures 9-12 is a modification of the idea in measures 1-4. Each leads to the B7 chord.

Melodic Variation

Use this variation in measures 15-16. Note the new chords. This variation would be most effective as an ending.

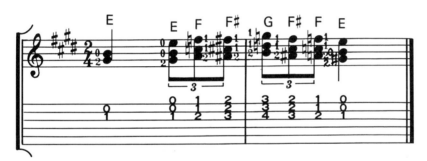

Oklahoma Stinger

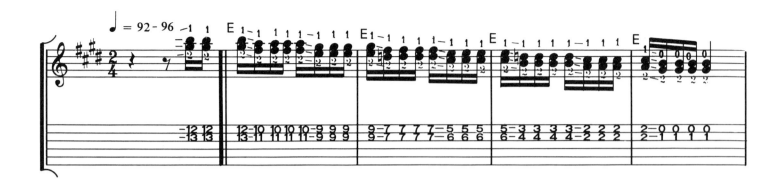

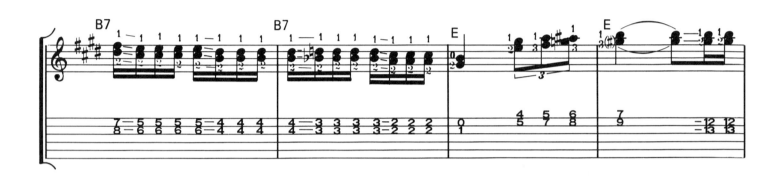

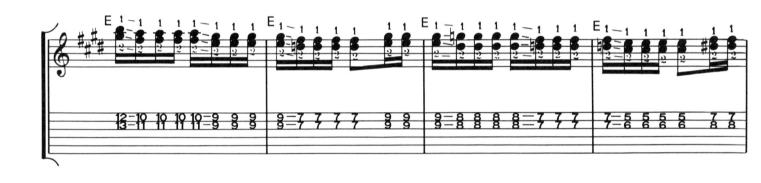

Texas-Size Heartache

* Measures one, five and eight each contain a "prebend and release" of a full step. Be sure to bend the note up to its proper pitch.

* A rapid double-pull is found in measure eight.

* The E note in measure nine is sustained into measure ten through the chord change from E (e, g♯ , b) to A (a, c♯ , e). This is a case of a <u>common tone</u> (to each chord) being held through a chord change, and is a concept you will undoubtedly find use for elsewhere.

* Note the position shift in measure 13.

* Note the use of the flatted third G in measures 15-16.

Melodic Variation

Use this variation in the fourth measure.

Texas-Size Heartache

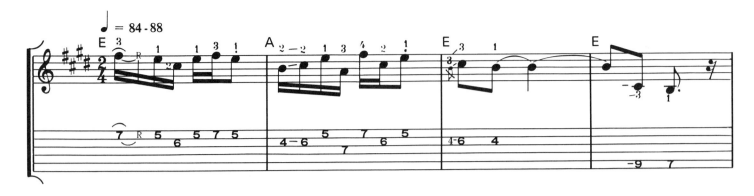

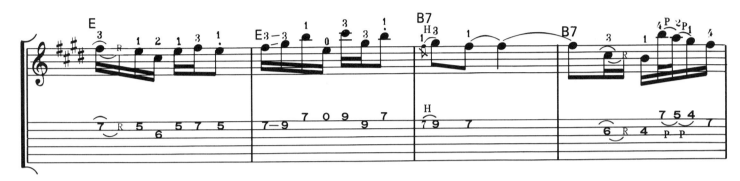

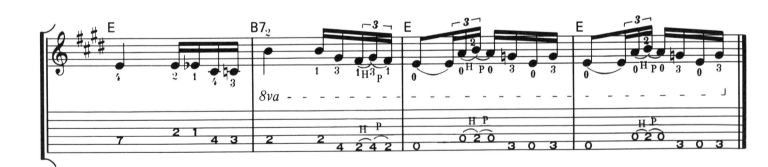

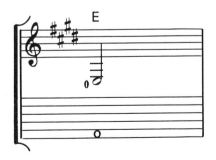

Trouble Up In Kansas

* Sometimes it's good to take a few moments to think of some of the concepts and techniques which are contained in a particular solo. A few used in this solo (which have also been used throughout this text) are:

* Delayed bends (measures 1, 7, 11).

* Stacatto notes (measures 2, 4).

* Flatted third (to the accompanying chord) blue notes (measures 2, 3, 14, 15).

* Use of a dominant seventh chord just before moving up a fourth, chordwise (measures 2, 4, 8, 14).

* Crosspicking (measures 5-6 and 9-10).

* Flatted seventh (to the accompanying major chord) blue notes (measures 5-6, 9-10).

* Various use of slurs such as pulls, hammers, slides.

Melodic Variation

Use this variation in the third measure.

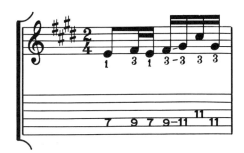

61

Trouble Up In Kansas

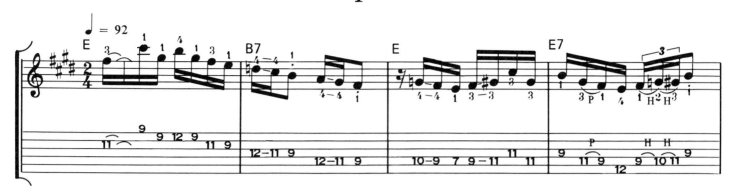

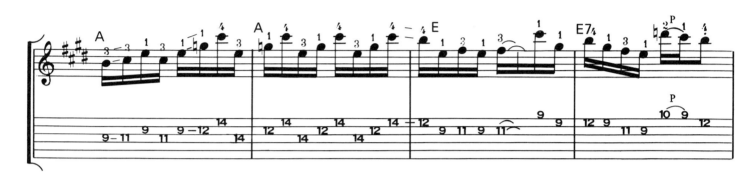

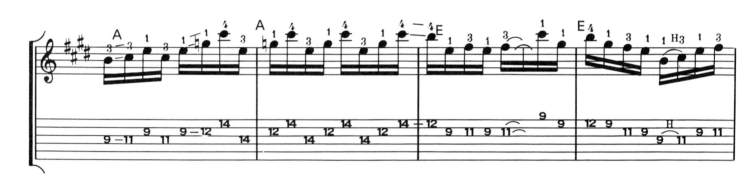

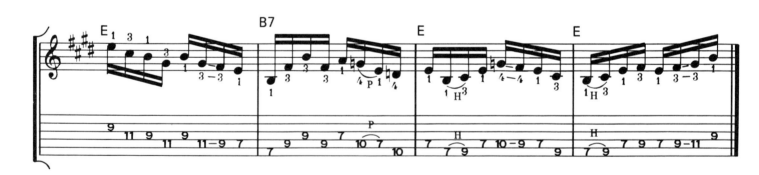

Egg-Yolk Sunrise

* There are many tricky spots in this 17-bar solo but the moderate tempo helps keep the fingering manageable.

* The first note in each of measures two and three is the major seventh tone of its accompanying chord.

* Note the manner in which the E major scale tones are used to build the ascending idea in measures 9-12.

* The doublestops in measures 12-16 may be played with the index finger on the first string and the middle finger on the second string. This requires a little extra stretching but allows for smooth slides. Play all the doublestops with a downpick motion for the best effect. See "Oklahoma Stinger" for a related study in the use of descending double-stops in the key of E.

* Measure seventeen contains a short lick using open strings which gives a ringing, steel guitar type of sound.

Melodic Variation

Use this variation in measure two. Only the last note in this variation differs from the version written into the solo.

Egg-Yolk Sunrise

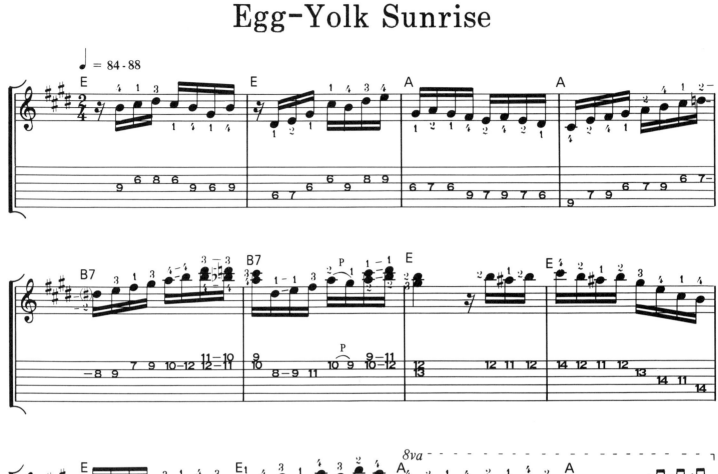

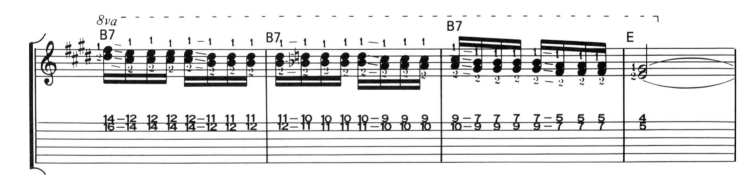

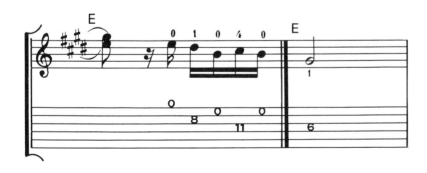

Cinnamon Sunset

*   Like "Navy Blues" (Key of G) and "Blues for Earl Haywood" (Key of D) this solo places heavy reliance on the blues scale. Historically, it has been common for country guitarists to incorporate the blues scale into their playing in a manner to make it "work" in country tunes. Anyone learning country guitar should listen closely to the early to mid-sixties work of guitarists Don Rich (of Buck Owens' Buckaroos) and Roy Nichols (of Merle Haggard's Strangers) to get an idea of the appropriate use of the blues scale and "blue notes" in country music. Any rockabilly music such as that of Carl Perkins tends to place great emphasis on the blues scale. Today, most guitarists like to add a little distortion when creating "bluesy" sounds.

*   The "Prebend and release" technique in measures one, eight and fifteen is described in the Symbols section of this book.

*   Note that successive downpicks are used on the final two notes in each of measures six and seven for the purpose of accenting.

*   Note that the open G string in measure seven is the flatted third tone of the accompanying E chord.

*   Measures 15-16 are the same as measures 1-2.

*   The solo-closing double-slide (following the final measure of the progression) uses a flatted seventh tone (d), intentionally creating a mood of unresolved dissonance.

Melodic Variation

Use this idea in the tenth measure.

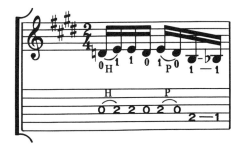

Cinnamon Sunset

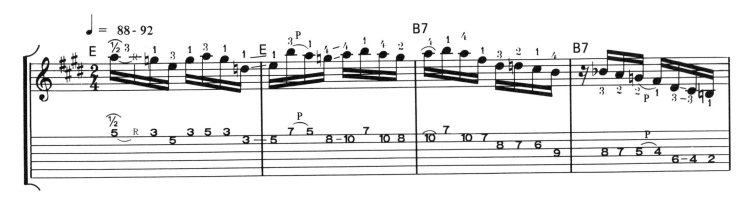

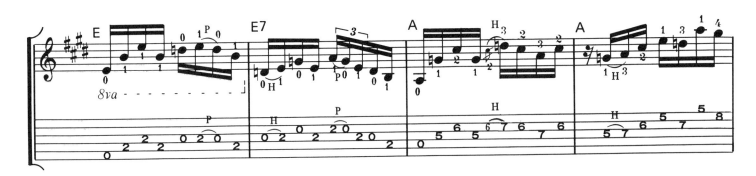

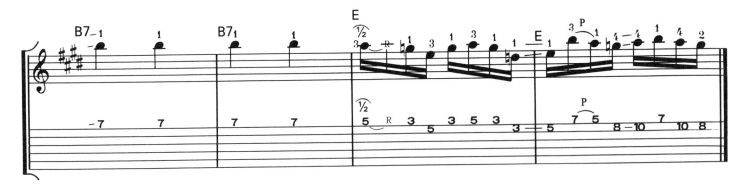

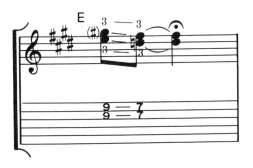

Elementary Music Theory

Music theory is essentially the study of the components or "ingredients" of music. Hundreds and thousands of "ingredients" related to time and sound are blended together by the human imagination to produce music.

If we are puzzled by music as though it were a foreign language, it may be because we lack the ability to recognize, understand and utilize its components. Logic tells us that we might begin to demystify music through the analysis and application of its various concepts and techniques. As in any artistic endeavor, we must understand in order to create. The more we understand about music, the more likely we are to experience it at the level of unlimited fascination.

This section of the book provides a basic view of certain theoretical principles related to this study. By no means is this information represented as being comprehensive--it is, in fact, just the beginning. Ask your music teacher, visit your music store, search through a university music library for the many fine texts devoted to theory. Of particular interest are theory texts which illustrate application of the principles. You may even consider taking a class or two if theory is offered through a junior college in your area.

The Circle Of Fifths

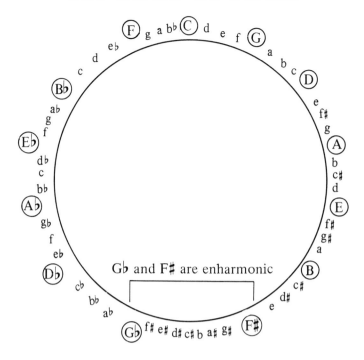

The "circle of fifths" displayed above is a visual aid used to identify various musical relation-ships. For our purposes we will use it for the following:

    1) Identification of major scale tones (and key signatures).

    2) Identification of the "three main chords" in each key.

    3) The spelling of the major and dominant chords.

Major Scale Tones And Key Signatures

Each of the songs in this book are played in one of the following major keys: c, g, d, a, e. Each of these keys uses as its tonal basis* a major scale which contains seven different notes. The scale and the key itself share the same lettername. For example, the cluster of notes known as the C major scale serves as the tonal basis for songs in the key of C major.

We may use our circle of fifths to "look up" the notes in any major scale by finding the letter name of that scale in a large circle and working clockwise until we arrive at the same letter (uncircled, this time) again.

Thus:

The notes in the Key of C are C-D-E-F-G-A-B-C (The C scale)

The notes in the Key of G are G-A-B-C-D-E-F♯ -G (The G scale)

The notes in the Key of D are D-E-F♯ -G-A-B-C♯ -D (The D scale)

The notes in the Key of A are A-B-C♯ -D-E-F♯ -G♯ -A (The A scale)

The notes in the Key of E are E-F♯ -G♯ -A-B-C♯ -D♯ -E (The E scale)

There are, of course, other keys. However, we are limiting this discussion to the keys used in this book.

*Simply stated, "tonal basis" refers to a given cluster of tones upon which the melody and harmonies of a musical compositon are based.

Key signatures are sharps and flats (or the absence thereof) written on the staff to avoid the unnecessary repetition of sharping or flatting of a note everytime it appears. Key signatures used in this book:

Three Main Chords In Each Key

Most of the songs in this collection use only three chords known as the "main chords" in the key they are used in. Thousands of country tunes contain only three chords. The three main chords in each key are labeled by the Roman numerals I-IV-V, because they share the same lettername of the first, fourth and fifth tones of the scale. Thus:

The main chords in the Key of C are: (I) C, (IV) F, (V) G.

The main chords in the Key of G are: (I) G, (IV) C, (V) D.

The main chords in the Key of D are: (I) D, (IV) G, (V) A.

The main chords in the Key of A are: (I) A, (IV) D, (V) E.

The main chords in the Key of E are: (I) E, (IV) A, (V) B.

We may use the circle of fifths to "look up" main chords without having to write out an entire scale. We can use the circled letters for this. Let's use the key of C for illustration. The circled letter to the left of C (F) names its IV chord. The circled letter to the right of C (G) names its V chord. Use this procedure to locate the main chords in any key.

The chord in the V position is often played as a dominant seven instead of major. Consequently, it is valid to make the following observations:

The V chord in the Key of C is (V) G or (V7) G7.
The V chord in the Key of G is (V) D or (V7) D7.
The V chord in the Key of D is (V) A or (V7) A7.
The V chord in the Key of A is (V) E or (V7) E7.
The V chord in the Key of E is (V) B or (V7) B7.

We now know how to look up major scales on the circle of fifths; we also know how to locate the three main chords in any major key. It is important that we also understand the basic substance of the scales and chords used in this book.

Scales And Scale Structure

A <u>scale</u> is a series of tones constructed (grouped together) with a specific, predetermined distance between each tone. The distance or "space" between the tones is known as the <u>intervals.</u> There are many types of scales; each is constructed according to its own unique plan. Any given type of scale will differ from other types because of the unique manner in which the individual tones are spaced apart in each type.

Three commonly used types of scales pertinent to this book are the <u>major scale;</u> the <u>blues scale;</u> and the <u>pentatonic scale.</u> Let's take a look at each one to see why they differ.

MAJOR SCALE STRUCTURE

Let us look at the major scales C, G, D, A, E to find out why they are all in the same scale "family" regardless of origin of pitch.

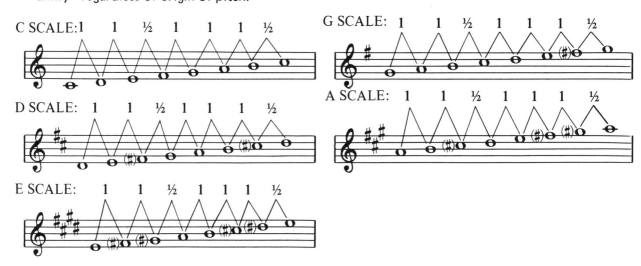

At the summit of each apex (Λ) is a number showing the stepwise distance between any two adjacent tones. As you can see, all adjacent tones in any major scale are separated by an interval of a <u>half-step</u> or a <u>whole-step*</u>. Visually (and aurally, as you play through the scales) it is apparent that all major scales are "alike" in the sense that <u>each is constructed according to the same overall plan.</u>

Many times a music student will ask: "If the major scale is the tonal basis for the major key, and if all major scales are alike in construction, why have different keys at all?" Several answers are listed below.

Avoid Monotony	It would get boring to play all songs in one key, just as it would get boring to paint all pictures using only one color.
Modulation	We often switch from one key to another (for dramatic effect, possibly) during a song.
Instrumentalist	A certain key is often preferred by the instrumentalist for ease of playing a given piece.
Vocalist	A certain key is often preferred by the vocalist for ease of singing a given piece.
Accidentals	The diatonic notes making up the scale give us the tonal basis for the key. However, accidental notes are often used to add "spice". Using only one set of diatonic notes would promote monotony and stifle creativity.

* A half-step on the guitar is the distance of one fret. A whole-step on the guitar is the distance of two frets.

70

Blues Scale Structure

The examples below show the structure of the blues scales C, G, D, A, E. Note that the blues scales are "alike" and of the same "type" regardless of origin of pitch.

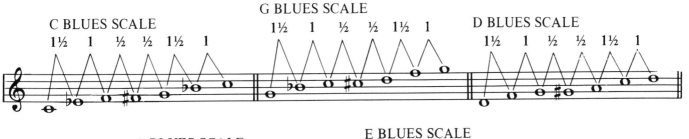

RELATION OF THE BLUES SCALE TO THE MAJOR SCALE

Because of its unique structure, the blues scale may be differentiated from the major scale (of the same lettername) by the following:

1. It has fewer notes than the major scale.
2. It omits the second and sixth tones of the major scale.
3. It contains both a "flatted third" and a "flatted seventh" scale tone from the major scale.
4. It has a "flatted fifth" tone from the major scale, as well as a regular fifth.
5. It can be distinquished in the auditory sense from the major scale.

Pentatonic Scale Structure

As its name implies, the pentatonic scale is a five-note scale. Like other "types" of scales it is unique in its own structure as can be seen below.

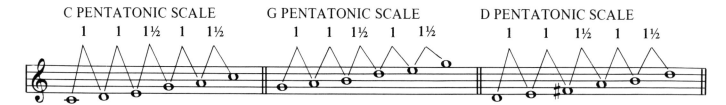

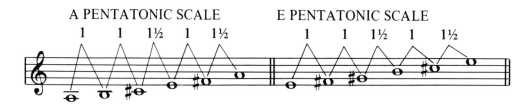

RELATION OF THE PENTATONIC SCALE TO THE MAJOR SCALE
(of the same lettername)

1. The pentatonic scale uses the first, second, third, fifth and sixth tones of the major scale.

2. The pentatonic scale has fewer notes than the major scale.

3. The pentatonic scale omits the fourth and seventh tones of the major scale.

4. The pentatonic scale can be distinguished in the auditory sense from the major scale.

Use Of The Scales

The three scales discussed in this book may each be used as a source from which melodies are created. Basic usage of each scale (in relation to this book) is summarized below.

1. The major scale is the most widely used resource in constructing melodies and harmonies (lead parts and chords) in the major keys. This is because the major scale itself furnishes the notes which are the tonal basis of the major key of the same lettername.

2. The blues scale is used as a basis for melodic ideas, but does not "establish" or "govern" a major key (as a major scale does). The blues scale often gives a "straining" (but pleasing, when properly used) sort of sound. The blues scale, as used in this book, will generally correspond to the key of the same lettername. Thus, the C blues scale us used when playing in the key of C; the G blues scale is used in the key of G; and so forth.

3. The pentatonic scale, like the blues scale, is used as a basis for melodies. In this book the pentatonic scale tends to be used in correspondence to the chord of the same lettername. In other words, we would use the C pentatonic scale (as a melodic basis) over a C chord.

By no means do any of the above statements presume to give a "complete" analysis of any given scale. Each summary merely reflects the general manner in which each scale is used in this particular book. The developing guitarist should make an effort to further study the construction, application and implications of scales. Two good sources for this are:

1. Jazz Guitar Lines by Vincent Bredice
2. Jazz Guitar Scales and Modes by Vincent Bredice
   (Both books by Mel Bay Publications)

Chord Structure

Chords (like scales) are grouped into different "types." Each type is built according to its own principle. Each basic type of chord (e.g. major, minor, dominant, augmented, diminished, suspended) is unique not only in structure but also in sound.
The melody we hear and play is strongly related to and influenced by the chord(s) which accompany it. For this reason the creative musician should develop a familiarity with chord structure.

This discussion will be restricted to the two types of chords used in this book--major and dominant. (Students are urged, however, to study the structure of all types of chords. I recommend Jazz Guitar Volume One by Ronny Lee, Mel Bay Publications.)

Major Chords (1-3-5)

To find the notes in any major chord simply start at the keynote (first tone) of the correspond -
ing major scale and locate the first, third and fifth tones of the scale. (The Circle of Fifths may
be used for quick reference.)

	1 2 3 4 5 6 7 8
C scale	Ⓒ D Ⓔ F Ⓖ A B C
C chord	C - E - G
G scale	Ⓖ A Ⓑ C Ⓓ E F♯ G
G chord	G - B - D
D scale	Ⓓ E (F♯) G Ⓐ B C♯ D
D chord	D - F♯ - A
A scale	Ⓐ B (C♯) D Ⓔ F♯ G♯ A
A chord	A - C♯ - E
E scale	Ⓔ F♯ (G♯) A Ⓑ C♯ D♯ E
E chord	E - G♯ - B

The numbers 1-3-5 are the chord formula. The chord spelling refers to the names of the notes
in the chord. The formula for any major chord is 1-3-5. The spelling for the C chord is C-E-G.
Major chords normally appear in sheet music as C, D, E and so forth without writing out the
word "major" after the lettername.

Dominant Seven Chords (1-3-5-♭7)

The dominant seven chord formula contains four voices. The formula for the dominant is like a major formula with a flatted seventh on "top." This extra note gives the dominant seven chord a unique sound quality distinct from the major.

	1 2 3 4 5 6 7 8	Flat seven
C scale	C D E F G A B C	B♭
C7 chord	C - E - G - B♭	
G scale	G A B C D E F♯ G	F
G7 chord	G - B - D - F	
D scale	D E F♯ G A B C♯ D	C
D7 chord	D - F♯ - A - C	
A scale	A B C♯ D E F♯ G♯ A	G
A7 chord	A - C♯ - E - G	
E scale	E F♯ G♯ A B C♯ D♯ E	D
E7 chord	E - G♯ - B - D	

Play a major chord and then a dominant chord of the same lettername. As you can hear, each has its own distinct sound. Dominant seven chords normally appear in sheet music as C7, D7, E7 and so forth without writing out the word "dominant."

Once the formula of any type of chord is known, its spelling may be looked up on the circle of fifths in this book.

Spelling Of The Main Chords In Five Keys

The chart below gives the spelling of the main chords in the keys of C, G, D, A and E major.

Key	I	IV	V	V7
C	(C)C-E-G	(F)F-A-C	(G)G-B-D	(G7)G-B-D-F
G	(G)G-B-D	(C)C-E-G	(D)D-F♯-A	(D7)D-F♯-A-C
D	(D)D-F♯-A	(G)G-B-D	(A)A-C♯-E	(A7)A-C♯-E-G
A	(A)A-C♯-E	(D)D-F♯-A	(E)E-G♯-B	(E7)E-G♯-B-D
E	(E)E-G♯-B	(A)A-C♯-E	(B)B-D♯-F♯	(B7)B-D♯-F♯-A

Elementary Melodic Concepts In Solo Work

Lead guitar solos like those in this book are basically melodies which sound good with the chords (harmonies) they are played to. The notes in the solo must more or less form an "alliance" with the chords so that both parts sound in "agreement" together. Three primary rules regarding solo construction will be discussed here.

1. The notes in the solo may be influenced by the tones in the accompanying chord.
2. The notes in the solo may be influenced by the scale tones which make up the key.
3. Accidentals (non-scale tones) may be used on a supplemental basis.

Example: Four measures in the key of C

       C scale tones: C-D-E-F-G-A-B-C

       Chords used: C(C-E-G); F(F-A-C); G7(G-B-D-F)

       Accidental tones: D♭ -E♭ -G♭ -A♭ -B♭

This example uses the diatonic I(C), IV(F), V7(G7) chords. As a result, the tones of all the chords in this example are contained in the C scale. Please take note of the following observations:

1. Eight notes are played in measure one to the accompanying chord C. Five notes belong to the C chord. (Notice that the measure begins on a chord tone.) Three notes (B, D, A) are in the C scale but are not in the C chord. No accidentals are used in this measure.

2. Seven notes are played in measure two to the accompanying chord F. Four notes belong to the F chord. (Notice that the measure begins on a chord tone.) Two notes (both G) are in the C scale but are not in the F chord. One accidental (A♭) is used to lead to the G7 chord in measure three.

3. Eight notes are played in measure three to the accompanying chord G7. Five of these notes belong to the G7 chord. (Notice that the measure begins on a chord tone.) Two notes (A, E) are in the C scale but are not in the G7 chord. One accidental (B♭) is used in this measure.

4. Five notes are played in measure four to the accompanying chord C. Three of these notes belong to the C chord. (Notice that the measure begins on a chord tone.) Two notes (A, D) are in the C scale but are not in the C chord.

These guidelines should be considered elementary rather than comprehensive. They are intended only to give the student a "roadmap" regarding the basic melodic aspects of soloing. These guidelines are a beginning, not an end. Each lesson in this collection highlights many solo concepts and techniques which supplement these basic observations. Through understanding and application of the principles detailed in this book, the student can go far in broadening his conceptual approach towards soloing and arranging.

WRITING YOUR OWN VARIATIONS AND SOLOS

The styles presented in this book sound best when played by a performer who has the ability to play the solos slightly different each time. Like most skills, this ability is developed rather than inborn. The following list gives a logical sequence one might follow in order to acquire such skill.

1. Learn a number of solos note-for-note.

2. Learn variations for certain spots in the solos.

3. Learn to interchange the variations at will (while actually playing) by thinking of them as "blocks" of notes which fit into a given time space in the chord progression.

4. Write your own variations. The two primary considerations here are:

      4a). Do the notes <u>sound</u> good with the chord they are played over?

      4b). Does the <u>timing</u> of the notes "fit" the space in the music you are trying to fill?

5. Write entire solos.

6. Interchange parts of entire solos.

7. Mentally create and technically execute spontaneous variations in solos (while actually playing).

Hopefully, this book has helped you satisfy #1 to #3 above. The following suggestions may help you as you work down the list:

1) Listen constantly to performers in the styles which interest you (but don't close the door on other styles).

2) Learn from technique <u>and</u> theory books.

3) Learn from recorded sources and live performances.

4) Learn from a good teacher.

5) Practice writing and playing your own parts (hundreds of them) constantly. Don't give up-if you do nothing will be accomplished ("I can't" often means "I won't").

Two assets possessed by all great guitarists are <u>individual desire</u> and <u>creativity</u>. When the desire exists, the creativity follows.

THE C MAJOR SCALE

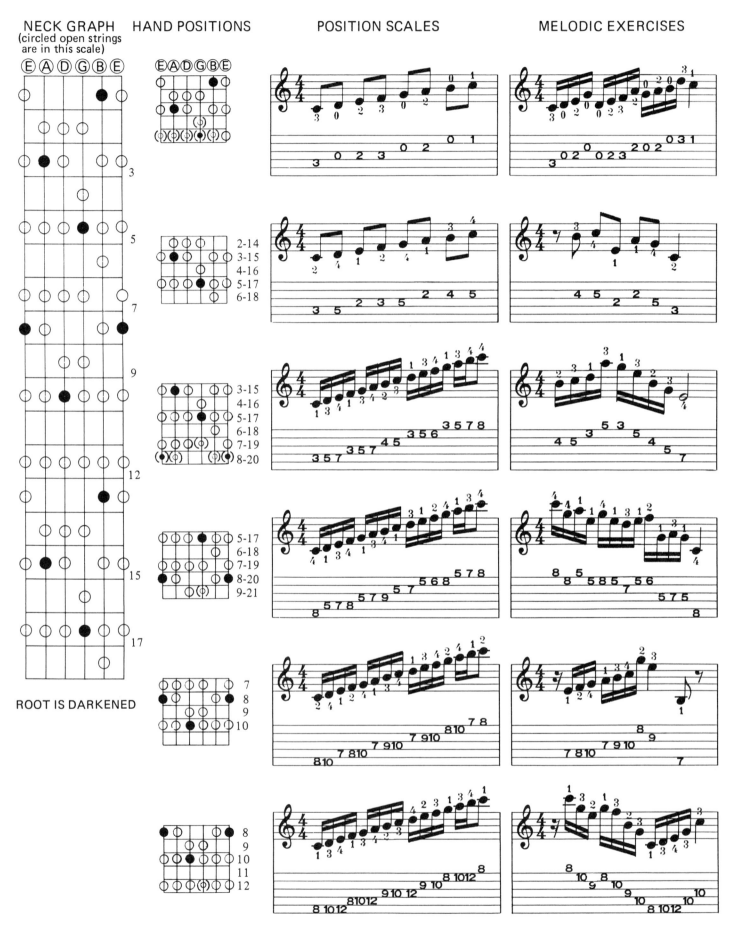

78

THE G MAJOR SCALE

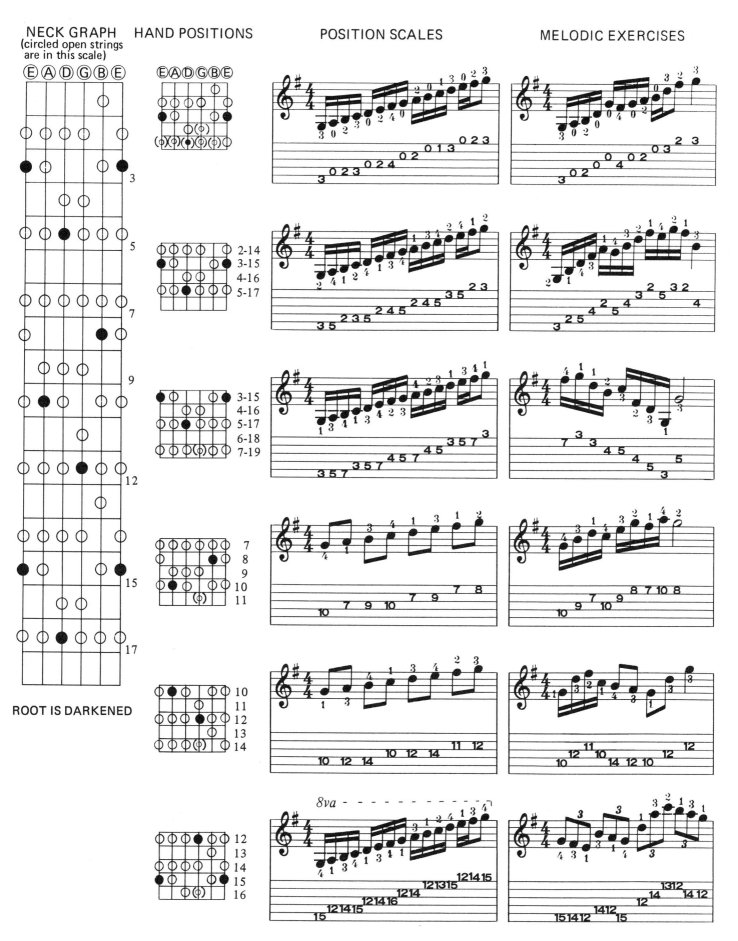

NECK GRAPH
(circled open strings are in this scale)

HAND POSITIONS

POSITION SCALES

MELODIC EXERCISES

ROOT IS DARKENED

79

THE D MAJOR SCALE

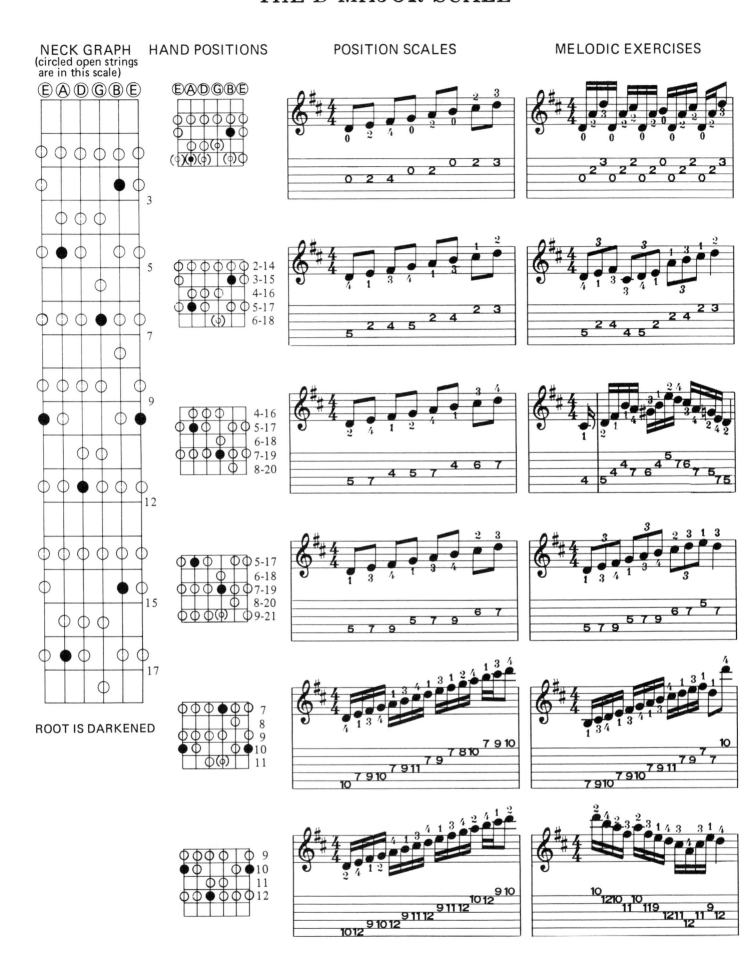

NECK GRAPH
(circled open strings
are in this scale)

HAND POSITIONS

POSITION SCALES

MELODIC EXERCISES

ROOT IS DARKENED

THE A MAJOR SCALE

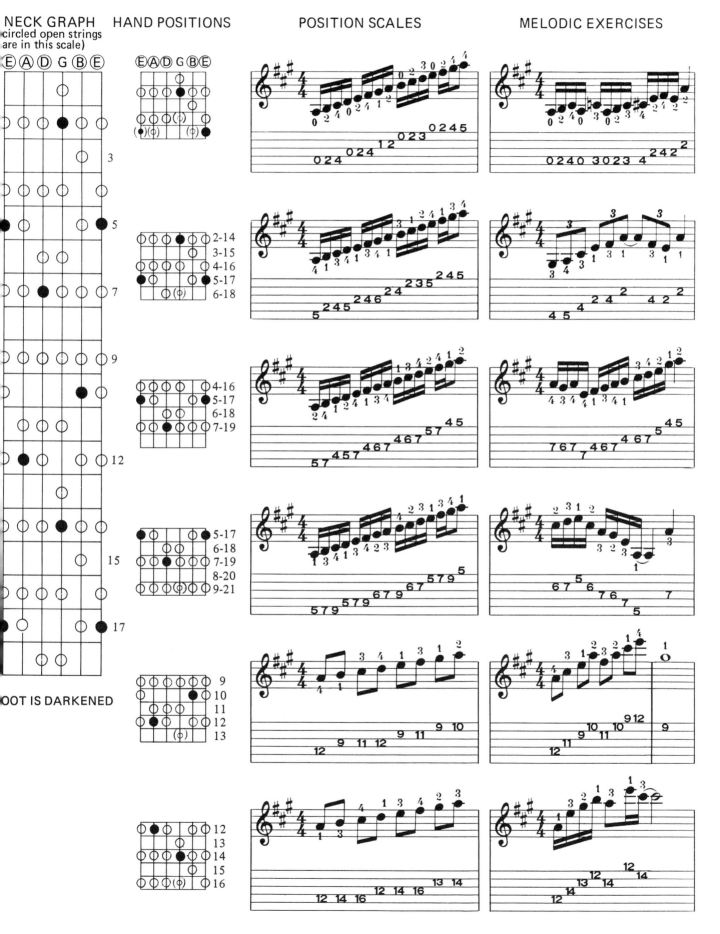

THE E MAJOR SCALE

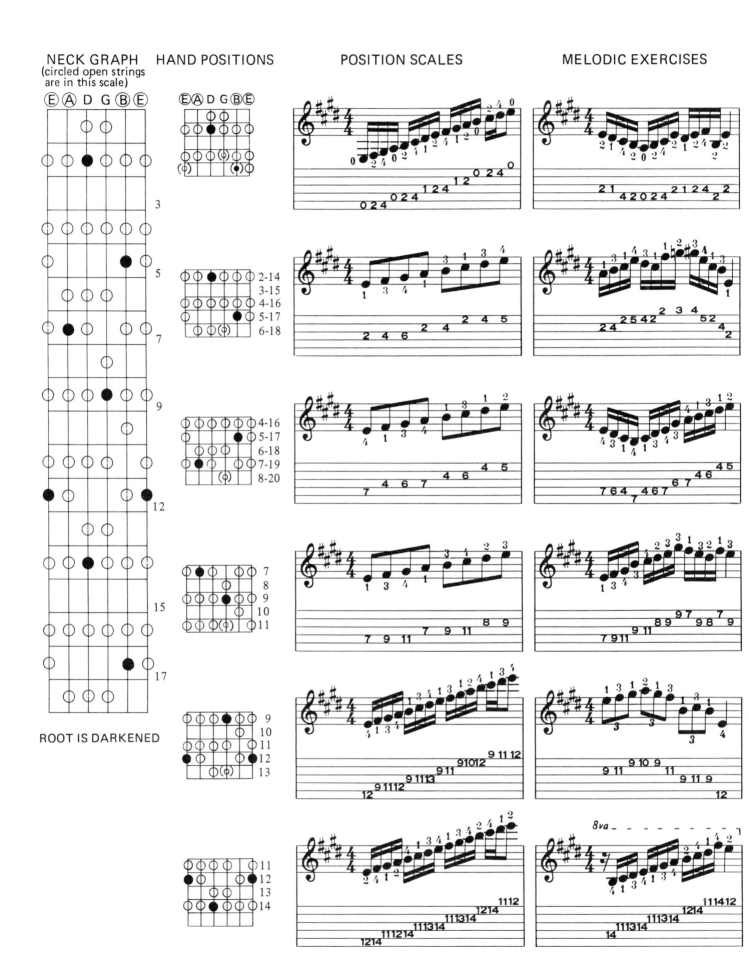

THE C BLUES SCALE

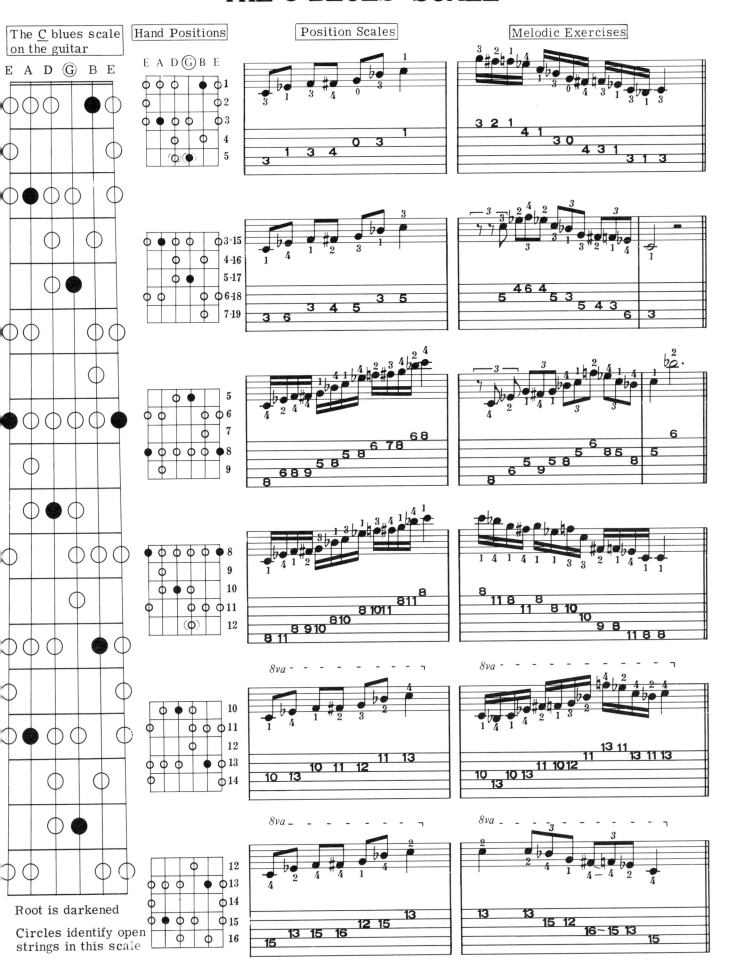

THE G BLUES SCALE

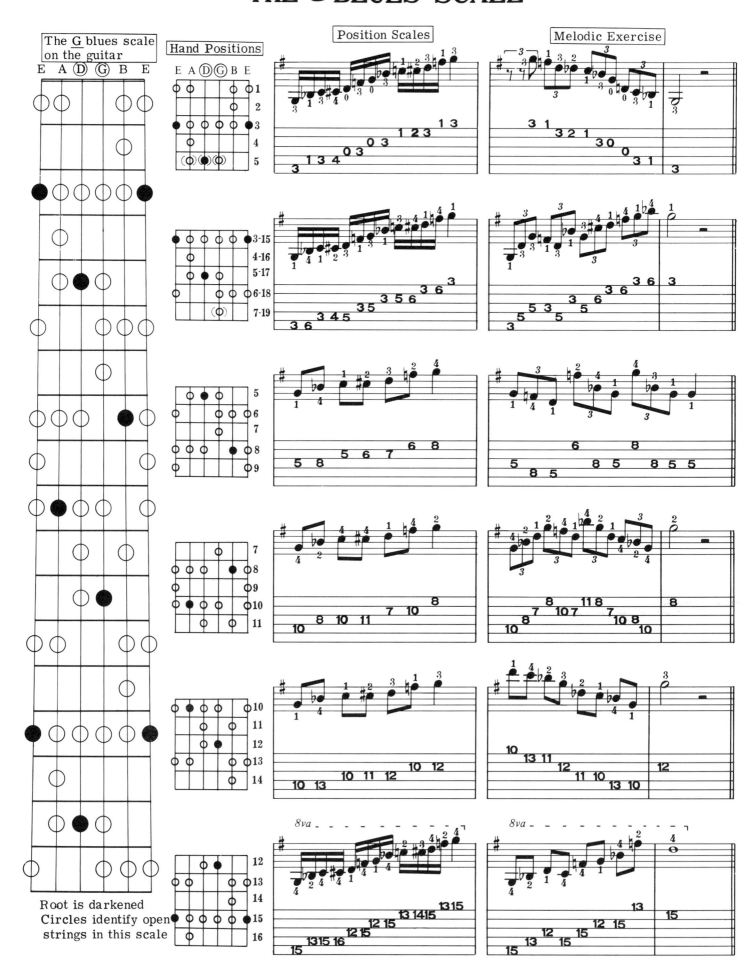

THE D BLUES SCALE

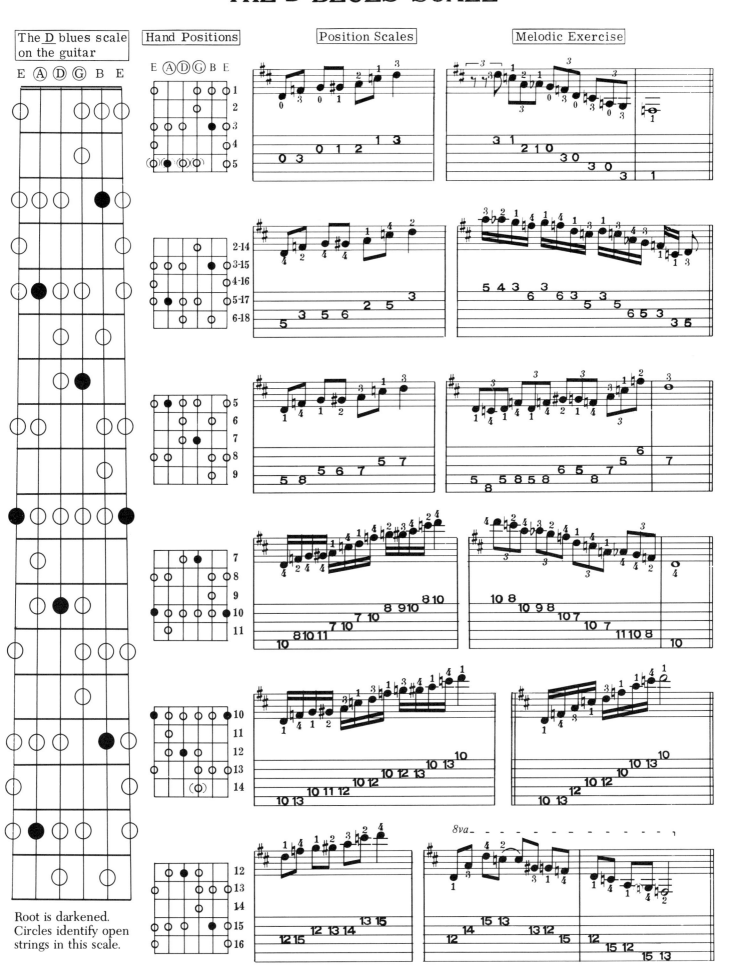

The D blues scale on the guitar

Hand Positions

Position Scales

Melodic Exercise

Root is darkened. Circles identify open strings in this scale.

THE A BLUES SCALE

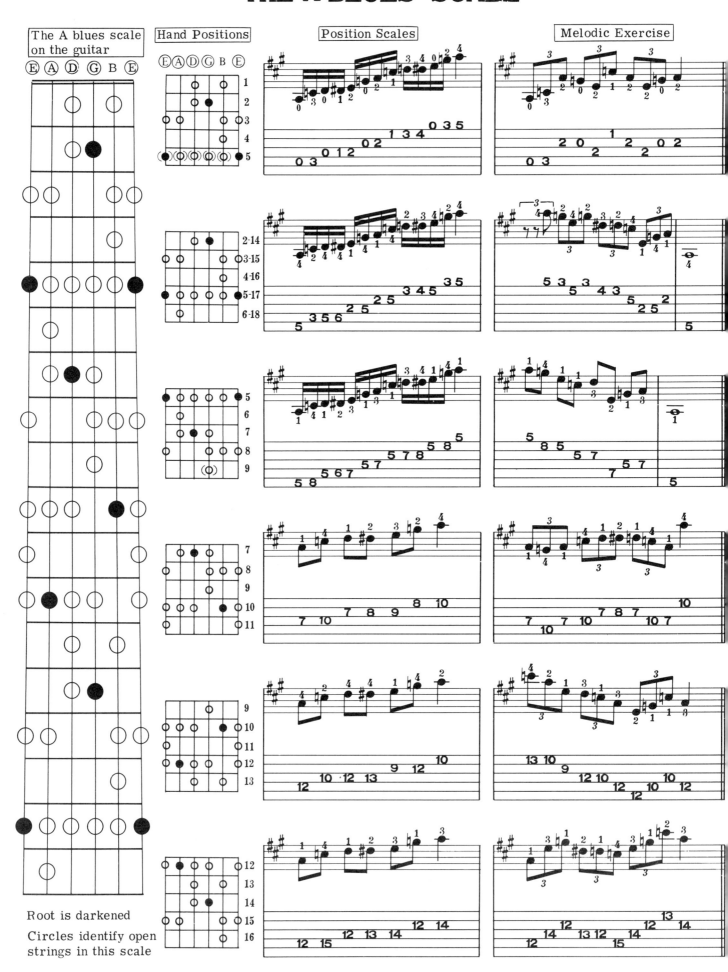

Root is darkened

Circles identify open strings in this scale

THE E BLUES SCALE

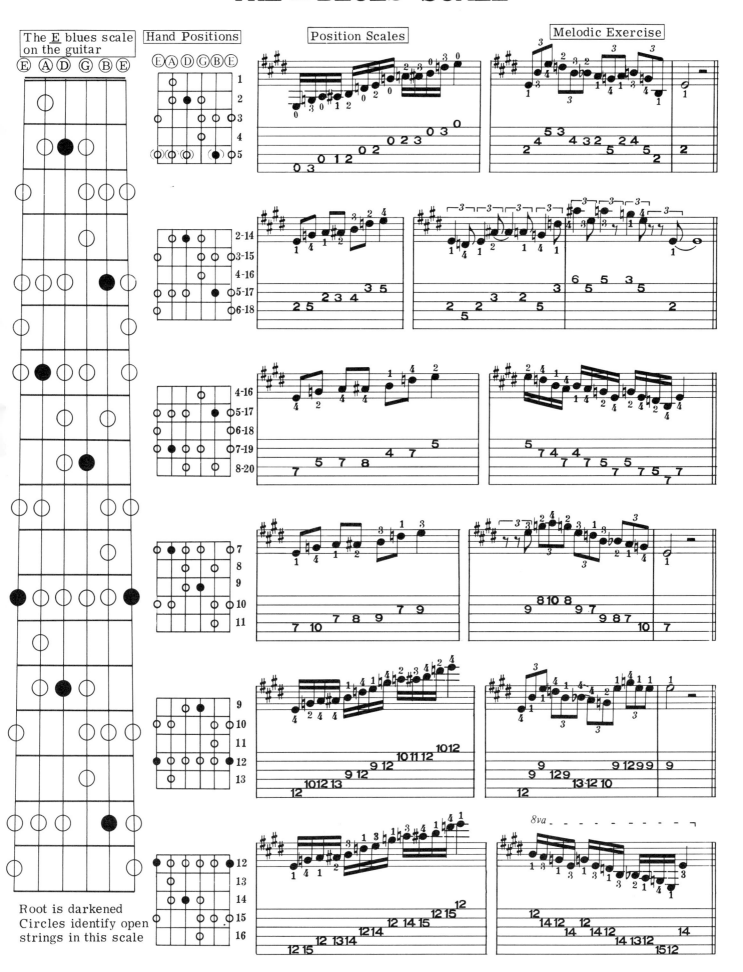

Root is darkened
Circles identify open
strings in this scale

THE A PENTATONIC SCALE

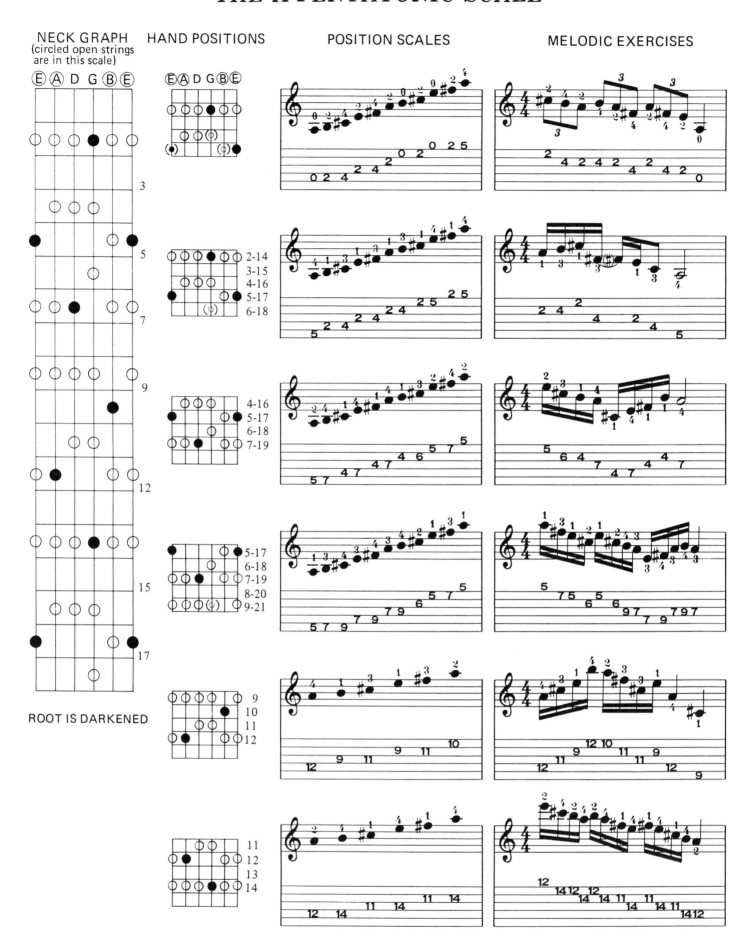

NECK GRAPH
(circled open strings are in this scale)

HAND POSITIONS

POSITION SCALES

MELODIC EXERCISES

ROOT IS DARKENED

88

THE B PENTATONIC SCALE

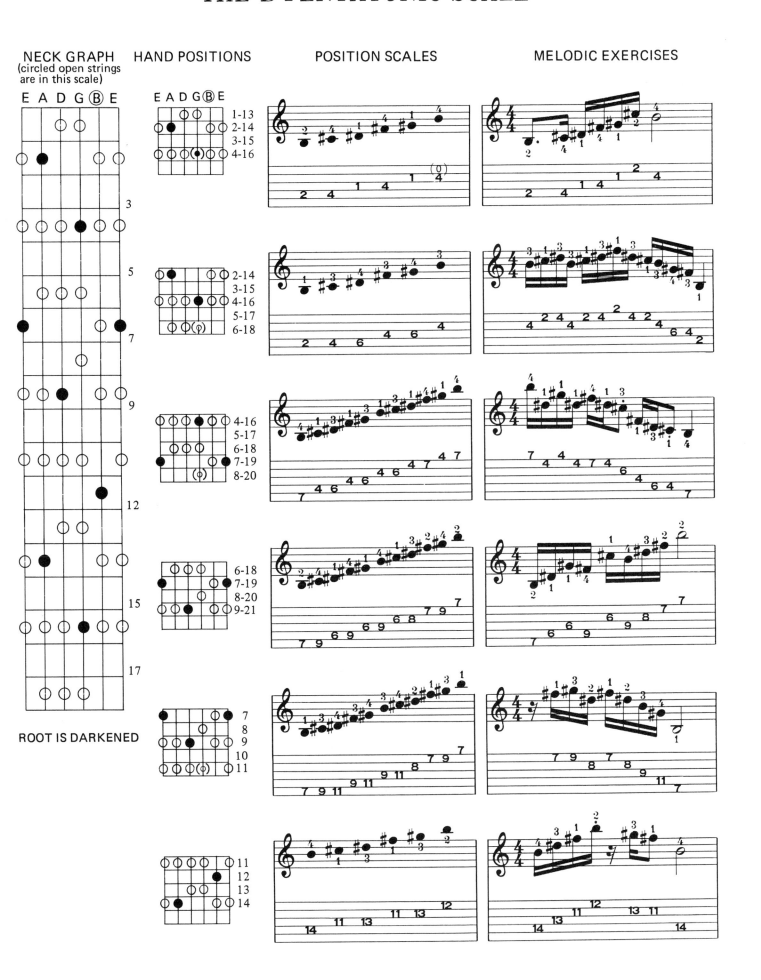

THE C PENTATONIC SCALE

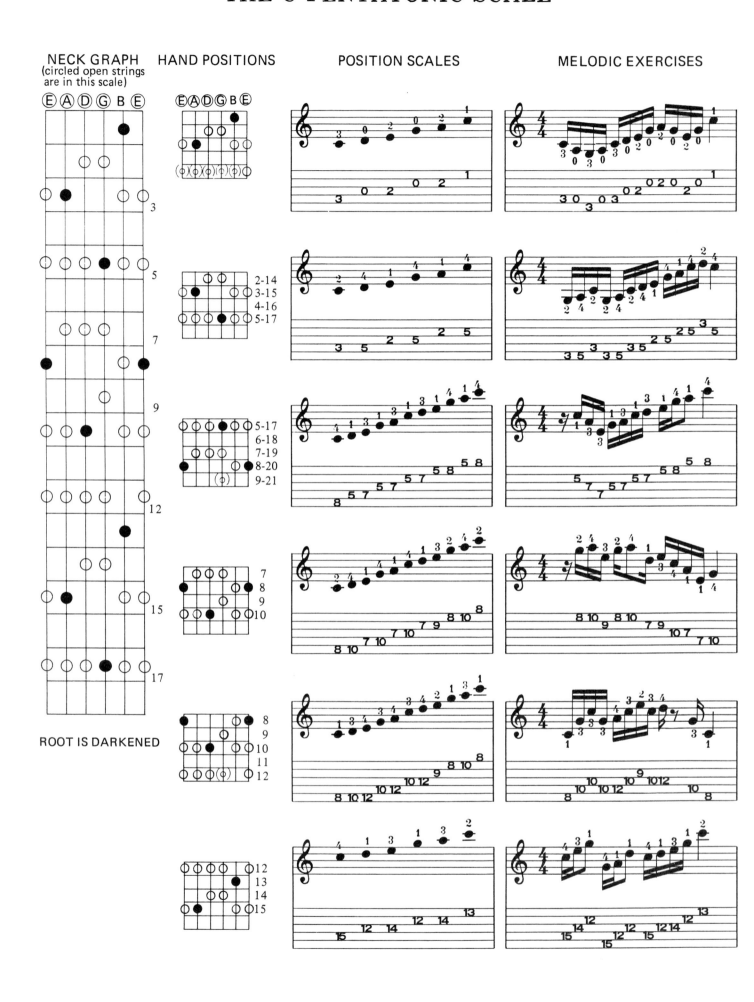

NECK GRAPH
(circled open strings are in this scale)

HAND POSITIONS

POSITION SCALES

MELODIC EXERCISES

ROOT IS DARKENED

THE D PENTATONIC SCALE

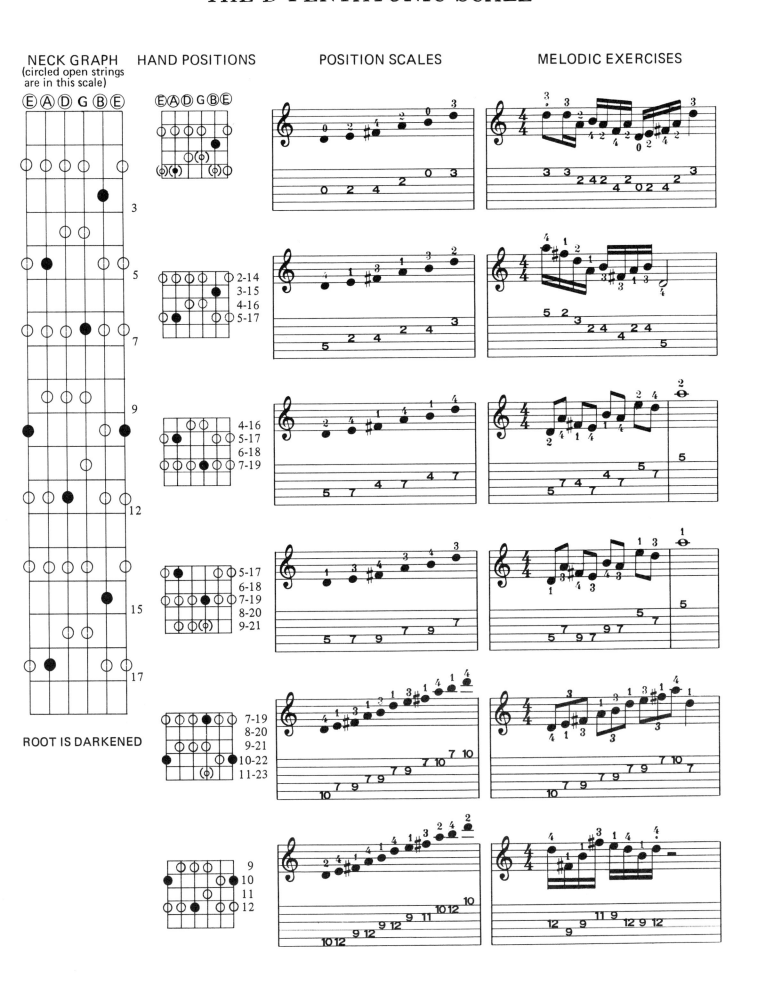

NECK GRAPH
(circled open strings
are in this scale)

HAND POSITIONS

POSITION SCALES

MELODIC EXERCISES

ROOT IS DARKENED

THE E PENTATONIC SCALE

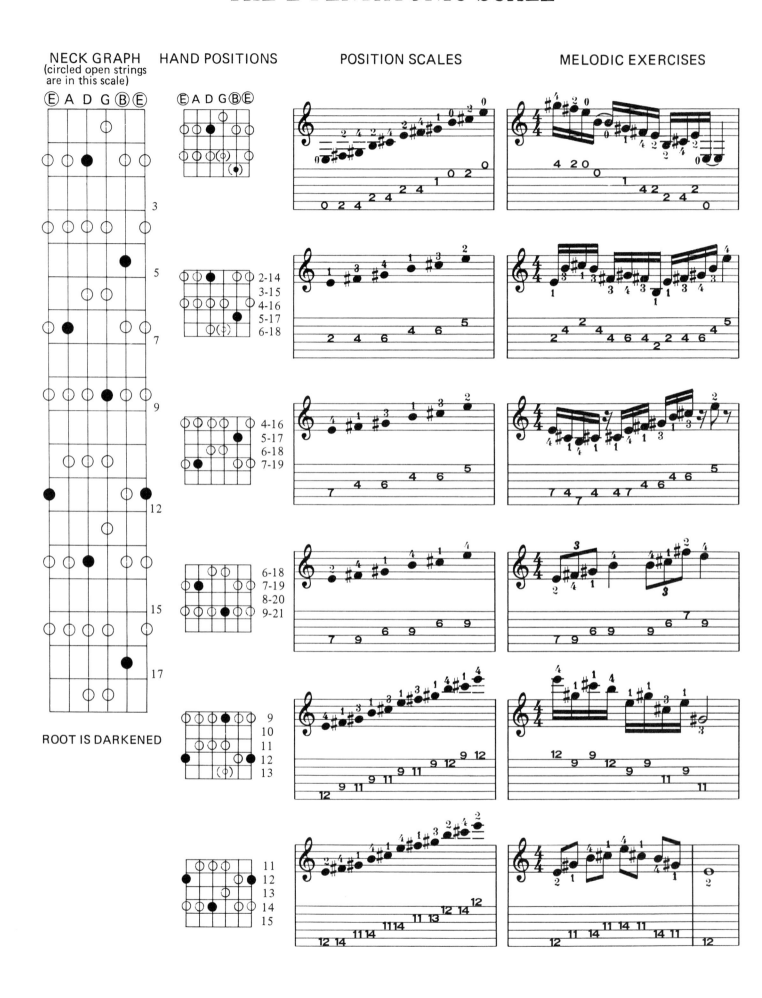

NECK GRAPH
(circled open strings
are in this scale)

HAND POSITIONS

POSITION SCALES

MELODIC EXERCISES

ROOT IS DARKENED

THE F PENTATONIC SCALE

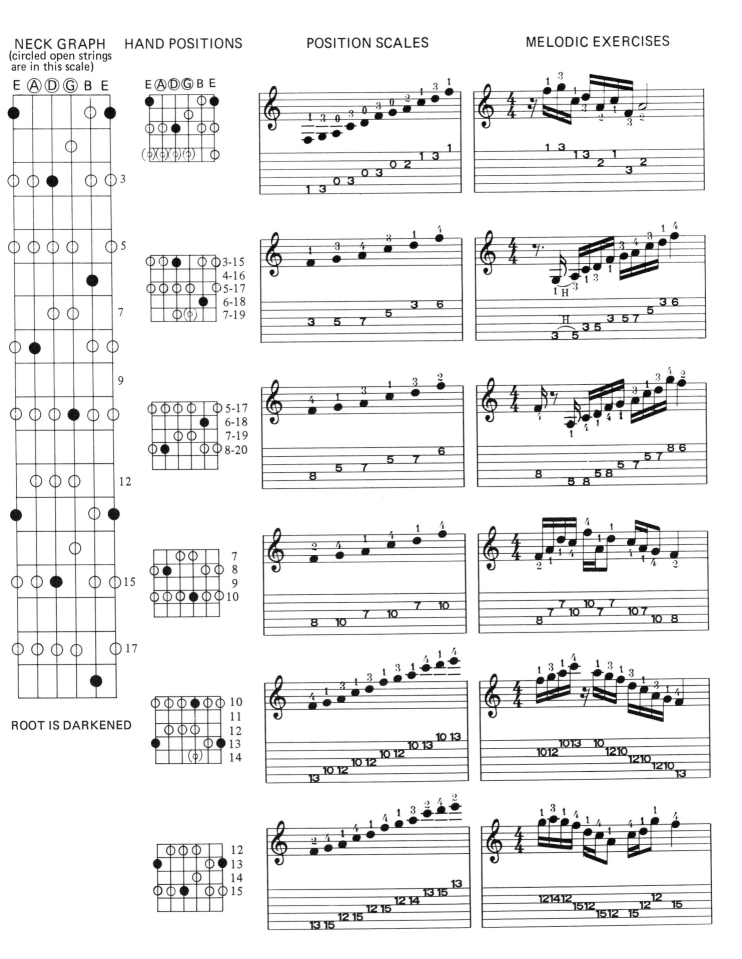

THE G PENTATONIC SCALE

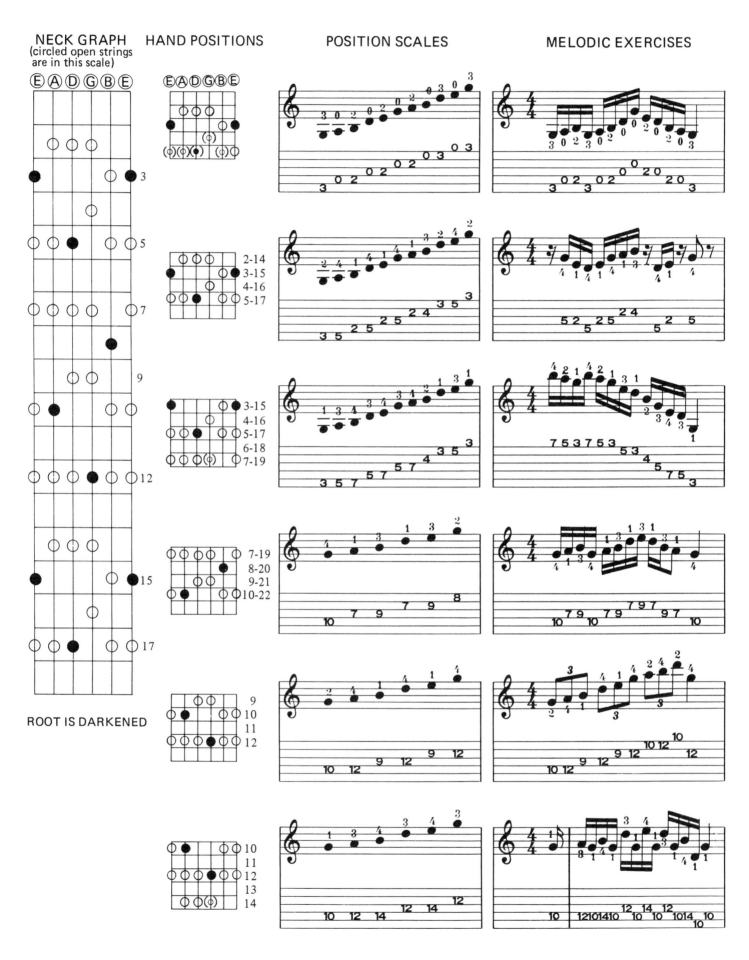

Everybody's Music Teacher